ALSO BY DR. ARTHUR S. SEIDERMAN

The Athletic Eye (1983)

20/20
IS NOT
ENOUGH

20/20
IS NOT
ENOUGH

THE NEW WORLD
OF VISION

DR. ARTHUR S. SEIDERMAN
AND DR. STEVEN E. MARCUS
IN COLLABORATION WITH DAVID HAPGOOD

ALFRED A. KNOPF　　NEW YORK　1989

This Is a Borzoi Book Published by Alfred A. Knopf, Inc.
Copyright © 1989 by Dr. Arthur S. Seiderman,
Dr. Steven E. Marcus, and David Hapgood
Illustrations copyright © 1989 by Dimitri Karetnikov

Library of Congress Cataloging-in-Publication Data
Seiderman, Arthur.
20/20 is not enough, the new world of vision / by Arthur S. Seiderman
and Steven E. Marcus, with David Hapgood.—1st ed.
p.   cm.
Includes index.
ISBN 0-394-57103-7
1. Visual training.   2. Vision.   I. Marcus, Steven E.
II. Hapgood, David.   III. Title.
RE960.S45   1989
617.7—dc19   89-45269
CIP

Manufactured in the United States of America
First Edition

CONTENTS

ACKNOWLEDGMENTS

Our first and greatest thanks go to those twenty-seven of our patients who gave us permission to use their own accounts of their or their children's experience with vision therapy. To protect their privacy, we have, with a single exception, identified them only with a first name and last initial.

The exception is Peter Borchelt, who appears in the text as "Peter B." We identify him here, with his consent, in order to thank him for his help with the content of Chapter 7.

Our very great thanks to Susan Harlem Maskin for help that was crucial to the writing of this book.

We thank Richard E. Cohen for his good legal counsel.

Our thanks to the staff of the Optometric Extension Program Foundation for their generosity in sharing their resources with us.

We would also like to give our thanks to our professional colleagues on whose work we have drawn in the course of writing this book:

Dr. Richard S. Kavner, friend as well as colleague, who is the author of two excellent books: *Your Child's Vision*, on which we draw in Chapter 3, and *Total Vision* (with Lorraine Dusky), on which we draw in Appendix A;

Drs. David Dzik, Roger T. Dowis, Joel Zaba, and G. H. Bachara, for their research on vision and juvenile delinquency, and Dr. Stanley Kaseno, for his account of his ground-breaking program in providing vision therapy to incarcerated juveniles, all of which we draw on in Chapter 5;

Drs. Glenn Corbin and Morton Davis, for their work in low-vision and vision therapy for older people, on which we draw in Chapter 8;

Dr. Joseph N. Trachtman, for his pioneering work in the treatment of myopia, on which we report in Chapter 10.

Finally, our warm thanks to our respective families for their support and encouragement: Susan Seiderman and our children, David, LeeAnn, and Scott; Ilene Marcus and our daughters, Melissa, Staci, and Jodi.

20/20
IS NOT
ENOUGH

1

VISION IN THE MODERN WORLD

Most people take their eyes for granted. Yet modern life puts enormous new stress on our vision. More and more, people in today's world are asking their eyes to do work for which those eyes were never intended. The human cost is very high. Consider these facts:

Millions of Americans see less well, use their vision less effectively, than they could. Millions of children's education is needlessly blighted by reading problems because no one bothered to ask if their vision was ready for the demands of school. Millions of Americans are a menace to others and themselves on the highway because no one has tested them for the visual skills that safe driving requires.

Many millions who earn their livelihoods doing close work find themselves hampered and held back by visual problems that go undiagnosed and untreated. Many older people give up their independence unnecessarily because of a visual problem about which they have been wrongly told "It can't be helped." And many more people function less well, and live less happily, than they would if their visual needs were met.

It need not be. The fact is that most visual disorders can be readily treated. In recent years, thousands of people who have been treated find themselves seeing better, working better, feeling better.

Even nearsightedness—that most common of eye problems—is now yielding to a new kind of treatment.

But millions of people with visual problems go untreated because most eye-care practitioners are unable or unwilling to diagnose and treat those disorders.

We know far more about vision today than we did when the current practices of eye care were developed. Since the 1940s, researchers have greatly expanded our understanding of human vision and our ability to help it function more effectively. But the practice of eye care has not kept up. With few exceptions, none of the new knowledge has entered into the daily practice of those who care for our eyes. Most eye doctors continue to practice along the lines set down long before we knew what we know today. While science has advanced, eye practice has stood still—at enormous cost to society.

The standard eye test is familiar to almost everyone. You sit in a chair and look across a room at a chart on which letters and numerals appear in decreasing size from the big E at the top. The eye doctor tells you to read as many lines as you can. If your performance is below normal, the eye doctor will ask you to look through test lenses until you are seeing normally in each eye. He will also test your eyes at close range. Depending on the results, he may write a prescription for glasses. He will examine your eyes for any signs of disease. In some cases he may recommend medical treatment or surgery.

What did that examination reveal? The chart on the wall, known as the Snellen chart (for its inventor, the Dutch ophthalmologist Herman Snellen), has remained essentially unchanged since the time of our Civil War. It was designed to find out if a child can see what a teacher is writing on the blackboard. It doesn't do much more than that, for discerning letters on a wall 20 feet away is not how most of us use our eyes.

The Snellen test does not answer the most important questions. It does not show if a child having trouble in grade school is visually equipped to read, for reading is a continuing process of seeking information at close range that is far different from making out the letters on the chart; still less does it tell us if an older student can handle the much greater reading demands of high school or college. The test does not tell us if the vision of an accountant or dentist or video-terminal operator is suited to doing intensive close work all day long. It does not tell us if a driver has the peripheral vision to see a car approaching from the side or the depth perception to tell how far away it is. It does not tell us if a young athlete's visual reaction time is good enough to save him from death or serious injury.

Those questions, which extend beyond the eye chart test to the entire eye examination, go unanswered because they are not even asked. They are excluded by the eye doctor's standard definition of his job. He offers a limited form of care restricted to the eyeball itself. If the image the patient sees is blurred, as in near- or farsightedness and astigmatism, he will prescribe glasses or contact lenses. He will not even examine how well the two eyes work together but will treat each eye as if it were an independent entity; the two lenses he prescribes might as well be prescribed for different people. Yet we are binocular beings. Binocular vision—the product of the two eyes working together—is what enables us to see in three dimensions and is essential to almost everything we do all day long.

As the traditional eye doctor sees it, there is nothing he can do for his patients beyond prescribing glasses and treating disease. His definition excludes the great majority of the visual needs of people experiencing the stress of modern life. That eye doctor does not ask, Can this person be helped to use his vision more effectively? Yet most visual disorders that now go undiagnosed can easily be treated. Much is now known about how people can care for their eyes so as to minimize the effects of intensive close work, and much also is known about the beneficial effects on vision of good nutrition. But the traditional eye doctor does not supply his patients with any of that information; it's not part of his job as he sees it.

By restricting themselves to the eyeball, the traditional practitioners are treating sight but they fail to treat vision. The difference is crucial. Sight occurs in the eyes alone. Vision is the interplay between the eyes and the brain. We humans are born with sight, but vision is learned. In our first days of life we can "see," but we cannot *see* in any meaningful sense because our brain has not learned how to see. We do not yet have vision.

Plato conceived of vision as a ray of light that we beam out from our minds to collect the images we see. As a metaphor, that is a pretty good description of what happens. Certainly it is far closer to the truth than the standard idea of the eye as a camera that presents fully developed pictures to the brain. What a camera! If one could photograph the images recorded by our eyes, they would appear as a hopeless jumble—and an upside-down jumble at that. Indeed, the eyes send the brain no images at all. Their information is conveyed to the brain not as pictures but as nonvisual electrical impulses carried by the optic nerves. From these impulses, the brain must reconstruct and interpret the eye's images.

The picture we see as we look out at the world is not in our eyes but only in our brains. That is where we give meaning to the eyes' messages. To take just one example, the eyes cannot interpret size, and so a fist held at arm's length appears bigger on the retina than a building half a mile away. It is the brain that on the basis of what it has learned in the past makes order of that jumble, that decides the building is in fact larger than the fist. By directing the eyes' attention, the brain decides what information it will have them collect, then decides what small part of that information it will notice and what meaning it will give to the information. That is why two people whose eyes have registered exactly the same messages may, and usually will, perceive what is out there quite differently. The same image collected by the eyes conveys a different meaning depending on the interpretation we place on it: a red light over a street means one thing, the same red light on a brothel quite another—to some, indeed, the latter is a green light.

Plato was essentially right: the brain reaches out and imposes its individual meaning on the collection of messages it receives from the eyes. Each of us creates his own visual world and it is unique. That is vision, and without it sight—the image in the eye—has no useful purpose.

When we say "I see a cow" we refer to our vision, not our sight, for our eyes don't know what a cow is. The brain scans the messages sent by the eyes to estimate size and shape, compares the result with images stored in visual memory, and concludes that what is out there is what it knows to be a cow. At the same time the brain matches those pictures to its memory of language to summon the spoken and perhaps written word that means "cow."

Vision is the window of the mind, the primary way we perceive the world around us. We are visual beings; sight has become overwhelmingly the most important of our senses. About 80 percent of the information that reaches us comes through our eyes. The volume of information collected by our eyes is astonishing. Each eye sends the brain a billion messages during every waking second. Together the eyes send twice as many messages as the entire rest of the body, including all the other senses. It was not always so. As our species has evolved, we have used our vision to extend our perception of the

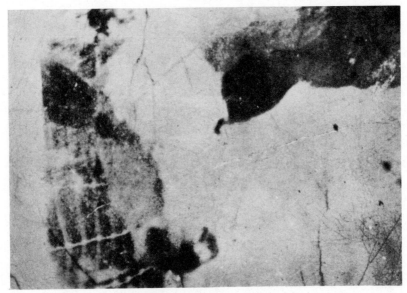

SIGHT AND VISION

What do you see? At first glance this photo seems to show only meaningless shapes. Vision is the process by which the brain organizes the information it receives from the eyes to give it meaning. Once that occurs, this picture will never again look to you as it did at first.

The photo shows a cow and is known as the "Renshaw Cow."

Photo courtesy of Optometric Extension Program Foundation

world past the reach of the more limited senses. Our ancestors even in relatively recent times had more need than we of, for example, the sense of smell, and species farther back on the evolutionary path depend primarily on other senses.

So dominant has vision now become that its messages overwhelm all others; our eyes send 430 times as many messages to the brain as do our ears. That is why we close our eyes when we listen to music. The sound is no different, yet we hear the music as fuller and richer when we shut out the overpowering messages of sight. Similarly, we often close our eyes to appreciate taste or smell. Our very language reveals the dominance of sight in such metaphors as "look into" and "foresight" and "vision" itself. We say "I see" to mean "I understand," while, if they could speak, a bloodhound would no doubt say "I smell" and a bat would surely say "I hear."

Our dominant sense so shapes our perception of the world around us, and therefore our behavior in that world, that in a large measure we are what we see, not what we touch or hear or smell. Our personalities are influenced by our visual perceptions: differing kinds of vision make for different kinds of people. Nearsighted people tend more than others to be loners, meticulous, shy, introverted. The outgoing personality is more likely to be farsighted. Because we learn vision in childhood, varying circumstances in the earliest years may make for different ways of seeing and so produce somewhat different personalities. A study by an anthropologist and an optometrist found that Chinese, who in infancy have a relatively restricted visual field compared to Americans, grow up to see more naturally and comfortably at a closer distance than do Americans. As adults the Chinese are more inward-looking; their perceptions and their attention are more likely to be concentrated in the area close to them.

Today the nature of modern life has placed an unprecedented stress on the dominant sense of vision by asking our eyes to do work for which they were not designed. Most people find that their eyes, when relaxed and free of any immediate task, tend to be more comfortable gazing off into the far distance than looking at something close at hand. There is good evolutionary reason for this. Distant vision was what mattered most to our remote ancestors. The necessities of life for which they searched—game and fruit and nuts—had to be discerned when they were far away. So did the enemies they had to avoid. Those among our ancestors who saw best at a distance were the likeliest to survive; they were the fittest. When, much later, our ancestors took up farming, they still depended mainly on distant vision. True, they did some close-up work—making tools, for example—but they did not need to see in fine detail, nor did they spend most of their waking day at it. And nobody read anything at all.

These realities remained essentially unchanged until very recent times. We invented writing, but only a minority acquired this new skill, and even of those only a very few spent their working days reading and writing. That was true of most societies (and is still true of some) until well into this century, which, on the scale of human evolution, is not even yesterday but more like an hour ago.

Now, in modern industrial society, and for the first time ever, the majority of people earn their living at tasks they perform less than an arm's length from their eyes. We spend our working days with our eyes focused at that short distance. For most people, their work involves reading—that is, interpreting small symbols on a printed page or, increasingly, on a computer terminal. Schooling, the gateway to success in modern life, which occupies us from age five usually into our twenties, is virtually synonymous with reading. What's asked of us, moreover, is not just knowing how to read, but how to read rapidly and accurately and for hours on end. If we can't do that, we'll fall behind the pack.

Spending our days working intensively at close range puts a heavy strain on eyes designed to search for distant game. Many people's eyes adapt by becoming myopic—nearsighted. Indeed, the prevalence of myopia is one of the surest signs of modernity. If half the people you see on the street are wearing glasses, you can be sure you are walking around in an advanced industrial society. For the evidence is by now overwhelming that, contrary to what is still widely believed, myopia is in most cases developed rather than inherited.

Among the many studies that make this point, two are particularly dramatic. In a survey of Eskimo families, among 130 children who were illiterate, only two were nearsighted, while of their peers who attended school, 65 percent were myopic. The difference was not inherited, for the parents and grandparents of both groups were equally farsighted. In Japan before the Second World War, the rate of myopia approximated that in the United States. During the war years education was neglected, and at war's end it was discovered that myopia among school-age children had dropped to half its prewar rate. After the war Japan recovered, education resumed—and so did the incidence of myopia.

Nearsightedness is only one of the effects of modern life on our visual system. Given the strains of functioning in contemporary society, it should come as no surprise that a great many of us have problems with our vision. The standard estimate is that 70 percent of Americans have less than adequate vision. This means that a majority of us get less than full use from our vital, dominant sense, the sense through which we primarily interpret what is around us. We are missing anywhere from a little to a great deal of what is going on, and we are responding accordingly.

Vision problems show themselves in many ways. For some, the effects may be mainly physical: the eyestrain, headache, and exhaustion experienced by people who do close work all day. For others, faulty vision manifests itself in missed opportunities, in a life that could be better. They could feel healthier than they do. They could do better in their work, be more successful in their careers, if their visual system functioned better than it does.

At first glance, visual problems may seem entirely personal, but in fact an individual's faulty vision can affect the lives of others in several ways. We all know about the huge numbers killed or maimed each year on our highways. All states require an eye examination in order to obtain a license, but in almost all cases it consists of nothing more than a test of distant vision on the familiar Snellen chart. Other visual skills essential to safe driving, such as depth perception, peripheral vision, and visual reaction time, are rarely tested in the United States (though some are tested in Europe). Surely many lives would be saved if all of us could see as well to drive as we can to read the letters on a motionless wall chart. Some children who fail in school because of visual problems will in time drop out and become delinquents who menace the rest of us. Society would surely be better off if more institutions emulated the California juvenile center where treating visual problems has dramatically reduced the rate of repeat offenses. Less familiar, and in its own way equally disturbing, is the frequency with which two radiologists will read the same X ray differently; sometimes a radiologist will even disagree with himself on a second reading—not a reassuring thought when a medical decision hangs on the outcome.

Athletes and sports fans are of course vigorous critics of the visual skills of officials. A Peter Arno cartoon of many years ago shows a minister rising in the stands to bellow in righteous anger: "Thou hast eyes but thou seest not!" That minister would no doubt feel vindicated by a study made of forty umpires and referees by one of the authors, Arthur Seiderman: He found that a surprisingly large proportion of them lacked normal vision. One-quarter of them failed to score 20/20 on the eye chart. Interestingly enough, a larger number had inadequate depth perception, a skill that is seldom tested, yet is essential to such work. Some officials had glasses but did not wear them at work for fear the fans would laugh at them. Visual problems can have far more serious consequences for the athletes themselves. Boxers and football players have died from injuries they could have avoided had they worked to speed up their visual reaction time.

In the past forty years, treatment methods have been developed and proven effective that can improve the vision of millions of people who are not helped by the traditional system of eye care. Those who have developed and who use those techniques are licensed professionals in eye care. Yet the great majority of their fellow professionals continue with methods of eye care based on doctrines that have not advanced in a century. Why do they refuse to adopt proven methods that would benefit many of the people who come to them?

In later chapters we will meet a variety of people who found another way to improve their vision. A few examples will illustrate the range of possibilities among those who have less than perfect vision. At one extreme is Peter B., an amateur race-car driver. He had no problems with his eyes. His vision was already excellent, better than that of most people; he did not wear or need glasses. "But I wanted the last one percent, because of the difference it could make on the racetrack," he said.

Brendan M. and Shari M. were at the other extreme. Brendan's visual disabilities prevented him from learning to read, and Shari's kept her from reading at the high school level. They were among the great number of American schoolchildren who suffer from a learning disability, or perform far below their potential, partly or wholly because of an untreated visual disorder. For both Brendan and Shari the problem was that their eyes did not work properly together as a team and so they found it painful to read for any length of time. But since they had passed the eye-chart test, their visual needs went unnoticed for too long. Both Brendan and Shari were headed toward failure in school and, almost certainly, in adult life.

Gretchen S.'s life was changed drastically for the worse in her forties when the onset of double vision not only forced her to give up her work but made such routine activities as reading and driving suddenly difficult. Two eye operations left her no better off than before.

Two other examples fall between these extremes. David H., an editor, was one of many people who are successful at doing intensive close work despite a moderate visual handicap. His disorder manifested itself in fidgetiness and lack of concentration at his desk, and eyes that felt tired by midafternoon. He did his work and did it well, but not as well or as quickly as he could have: he scored perhaps a B− rather than his potential B+. Libby K.'s visual disorder was fairly severe, but in compensation her life as an adult made relatively mild demands on her vision. Her trouble manifested itself in mishaps during routine tasks—she bumped into kitchen cabinets and she drove her car up on the curb too often for these things to be merely accidental—and she didn't read even the newspaper because it was too much work.

These six stories all have happy endings, as we will see in greater detail in later chapters. Peter is doing better on the racetrack. "Now time moves more slowly in a race," he says. "My car and the other cars—the whole track seems to be moving in slow motion." Brendan, who could not learn to read in second grade, won a reading prize the next year and eventually went on to an Ivy League college. Shari, flunking in her freshman year, got A's and B's as a sophomore. "I love school now," she said that second year. "My friends think I'm smart." Gretchen's vision is getting steadily better, despite the effects of two needless operations. David, the editor, gets more and better work done each day with less discomfort; even his tennis has improved within the limits of the possible. Libby finds she gets through her days far more comfortably. "I'm not so nervous now," she says. "I don't bump into things."

What made the difference is the process known as vision therapy.

EVALUATING YOUR VISION

What follows are two sets of questions designed to help the reader judge the state of his or her own vision. The first set of ten questions describes major signs of a problem in one's vision. If you answer yes to any of these first ten questions, we believe you should get a full examination by an eye doctor who tests the skills of vision as well as sight. (For finding such an eye doctor, see the box on p. 20.)

1. Do your eyes hurt?
2. Do you see double?
3. Does your vision blur when you look to the distance, or when you are doing close work?
4. Do your eyes water a lot?
5. Do your eyes get very bloodshot?
6. Do you get headaches after intense visual activities such as reading or driving?

7. Do you feel dizzy or sick to your stomach after intensive close visual activity such as working at your desk?
8. Do you see more clearly with one eye than with the other?
9. Do you ever see flashes of light?
10. Is part of your field of vision missing in one or both eyes?

The following, much longer, list is of less severe signs of possible visual problems. We believe you should consider a full visual examination if you answer yes to between five and ten of these questions. If you answer yes to more than ten questions, then we suggest you promptly seek such an examination.

1. Do your eyes tire quickly when you are reading or working at a video display terminal?
2. Does your comprehension tend to decrease the longer you read?
3. While reading do you confuse similar words or letters?
4. While reading do you skip words?
5. While reading do you lose your place?
6. Do you read very slowly?
7. Do you read word by word?
8. Do you often have to reread a line you've just read?
9. When reading do you sound words aloud or move your lips silently?
10. Do you use your finger or a marker to keep your place while reading or writing?
11. Do you have difficulty remembering what you've read?
12. Does your mind wander when you're reading?
13. Do you avoid reading?
14. Do you hold your head very close to what you're reading or writing?
15. Do you turn your head a great deal while reading or working at a computer?
16. Do you rub your eyes frequently after or while reading or working at a computer?
17. Do you tilt your head to one side to read?
18. Do you turn your head so you are using only one eye?
19. Do you close or cover one eye?
20. Do you write neatly but very slowly?
21. Do you have trouble with spelling?
22. Do you often reverse letters, words, or numbers?
23. Are you restless when working at your desk?
24. Does your distance vision blur when you look up from close work?

25. Do you lose visual clarity when you concentrate?
26. Do you do poorly on standardized tests?
27. Do you have difficulty with written directions or instructions?
28. Do you dislike tasks requiring sustained visual attention?
29. Do lights bother your eyes?
30. Do you avoid close work?
31. Do you feel unusually tired after you complete a visual task?
32. Do you feel nervous, irritable, restless, or frustrated after sustained visual concentration?
33. Do you learn better from listening than from seeing?
34. When concentrating do you tend to lose awareness of your surroundings?
35. Do you daydream a lot?
36. Do you frequently trip or stumble?
37. Do you have trouble threading a needle?
38. Do you find it difficult to see another person's point of view?
39. Do you find it difficult to visualize an action and its consequences before you take it?
40. Do you blink a lot?
41. Do you have frequent sties?
42. When talking to people, do you avoid eye contact?
43. Do you find it hard to remember people's faces?
44. Do you find it difficult to use binoculars?
45. Do you feel uncomfortable in a crowded area with a lot of movement such as a shopping mall, terminal, or department store?
46. Do you have trouble reading a map?
47. Do you tailgate when driving?
48. Do you have trouble judging distance while parking?
49. Do you find night driving difficult?
50. Do you get carsick?
51. Are eye-hand–coordination sports such as tennis, racquetball, and baseball difficult for you?
52. Are eye-body–coordination activities such as dancing difficult for you?

2

VISION THERAPY

The retina divides the old from the new in the practice of professional eye care.

This thin membrane at the back of the eyeball is where sight and vision meet. The retina is where light that has entered the eye at the cornea and been focused by the lens is transformed into electrical messages to be sent to the brain.

We eye doctors who practice vision therapy are primarily concerned with what happens *behind the retina*, in the interaction between brain and eyes—the world of vision.

Traditional eye care is limited to what happens *in front of the retina* —the world of sight. Its practitioners treat what are called "refractive errors," of which the most common are, as we have observed, myopia (nearsightedness), hyperopia (farsightedness), and astigmatism—all of which are due to an improperly shaped eyeball. The improper shape prevents the image focused by the lens from falling accurately on the retina. If the eyeball is elongated from front to back, the distance from lens to retina is too great, and the image focuses before the retina; the result is myopia. If the eyeball is too shallow, the focus falls beyond the retina, and that is farsightedness. Astigmatism is due to an irregularly shaped eyeball that distorts the focus. All three are readily treated by eyeglasses or contact lenses that compensate for the effects of the misshapen eyeball and cause the image to fall accurately on the retina. Such prescribing, plus in some cases medical or surgical treatment, is the self-imposed limit of traditional eye practice.

HOW THE EYE WORKS

Light enters the eye through the cornea, the fluid-filled bulge at the front of the eyeball. The cornea slows down the light and bends it toward the center. The light now reaches the iris, which narrows or expands the dark hole at its center, the pupil, to regulate the amount of light that proceeds toward the retina. The pupil narrows in bright light, dilates when light is dim. The lens focuses the light when its shape is changed by the ciliary muscle; this sharpens the picture the lens has received from the cornea. To reach the retina, the image now passes through the ball of clear jelly that makes up the greater part of the eye. This "vitreous humor" exerts fluid pressure that maintains the eyeball's shape. (Occasional vague shapes we see before our eyes are dead blood cells floating in the jelly.) The retina is a thin membrane at the back of the eyeball. The macula, a small area near the center of the retina, is the region of greatest visual acuity. And sight is keenest of all at the fovea, the tiny pit at the center of the retina. When we turn our eyes toward what we want to look at, we are aligning them so that light falls directly on the fovea. The retina is where the image first recorded by the cornea and modified along the way is translated into electrical messages carried by the optic nerves to those parts of the brain where we interpret what our eyes record.

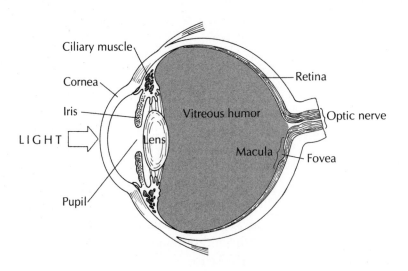

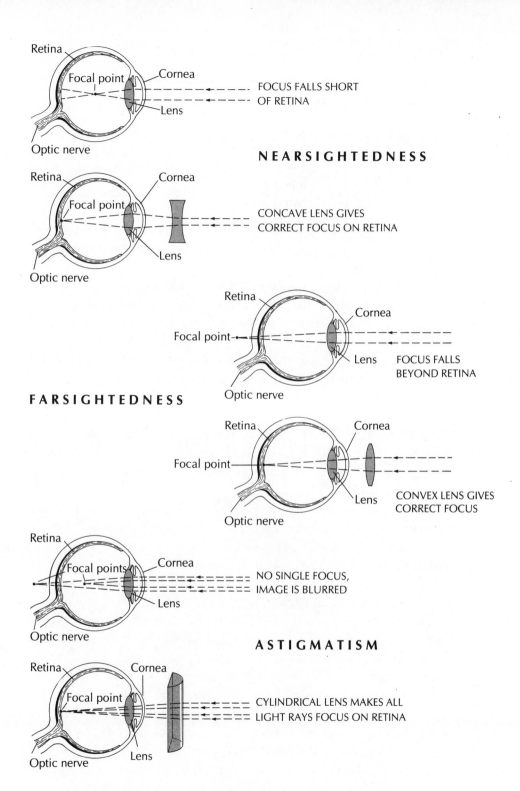

Retina
Focal point
Cornea
Lens
Optic nerve

FOCUS FALLS SHORT
OF RETINA

NEARSIGHTEDNESS

Retina
Focal point
Cornea
Lens
Optic nerve

CONCAVE LENS GIVES
CORRECT FOCUS ON RETINA

Retina
Cornea
Focal point
Lens
Optic nerve

FOCUS FALLS
BEYOND RETINA

FARSIGHTEDNESS

Retina
Cornea
Focal point
Lens
Optic nerve

CONVEX LENS GIVES
CORRECT FOCUS

Retina
Focal points
Cornea
Lens
Optic nerve

NO SINGLE FOCUS,
IMAGE IS BLURRED

ASTIGMATISM

Retina
Cornea
Focal point
Lens
Optic nerve

CYLINDRICAL LENS MAKES ALL
LIGHT RAYS FOCUS ON RETINA

HOW LENSES CORRECT REFRACTIVE ERROR

Developmental optometry, as our specialty is called, is concerned not just with how well people see but with how well they are able to use their eyes and how comfortably they can sustain visual concentration. We believe that good sight—a score of 20/20 on the eye chart—is not enough; the person must also have the ability to make full use of his vision. The purpose of vision therapy is to remedy those visual disorders that prevent people from enjoying that full use of vision.

The symptoms of visual disorders show up in the eyes, but their causes lie elsewhere. The problems are found in the interpretation by the brain of the messages it gets from the eyes and in the instructions it gives the eyes.

The most visible and familiar disorder of vision is known as strabismus, which means that one or both eyes are turned, sometimes up or down but usually in or out: the person is cross-eyed or walleyed. Amblyopia, or lazy eye, is a related problem but is less obvious than strabismus. One eye sees but does not function properly in conjunction with its partner, so the brain suppresses its messages and in effect gets along with the information supplied by the other eye.

Orthoptics, the precursor of today's vision therapy, had its origins in the treatment of strabismus in the late nineteenth century. The French ophthalmologist Emile Javal developed a series of training routines as an alternative to eye surgery after seeing the results of operations performed on both his father and his sister, operations which he described as *"le massacre des muscles oculaires."* Today some practitioners still treat strabismus with surgery, though the success rate is only 20 percent, compared to the 70 percent achieved by vision therapy. "Success" in this case means that the two eyes function effectively together. Surgery may correct the appearance of the eye without assuring good visual functioning.

Disorders of "binocular fusion" involve difficulties in using the eyes as a team. Binocular vision is a complex process involving several sets of nerves and muscles. All we are aware of is that with our conscious mind we tell our eyes to direct their attention to the so-called object of regard. The response seems to us immediate but involves several successive actions ordered by the brain: it tells one set of muscles to turn the eyes in or out, instructs other muscles to bring the eyes together so that the image falls on the center of each retina, then to fuse the two images into one, and finally tells a muscle in each eyeball

FIGURE VERSUS GROUND

In this drawing you can see either an old woman or a young one. You can see them alternately, but you cannot see them both at the same time. This is how the brain achieves visual concentration. By organizing visual information to perceive one representation—the figure—it temporarily excludes competing information—the ground. People who have difficulty with figure-ground discrimination are likely to have trouble concentrating on written information. For example, a child looking at a page full of arithmetic problems may find it hard or impossible to concentrate visually on one problem to the exclusion of the others. This picture was devised by the psychologist E. G. Boring and is known as "Wife/mistress."

to adjust the lens to focus the image. A malfunctioning in any of these systems will make binocular vision difficult to achieve and especially difficult to sustain. Unlike cross-eyes or walleyes, these disorders are not immediately visible. They manifest themselves most often when a person has trouble with that most necessary and visually demanding task of modern life, reading, and similar kinds of concentrated work. Reading with such a disorder will be uncomfortable and sometimes painful.

Since, as noted, the causes of all visual disorders lie in the messages sent by the brain to the eye, that is also where the cure takes place. Vision is learned, and in therapy the brain learns to do it better. Vision therapy trains the brain to give the correct instructions to the muscles of the eye. The instruments we use are designed to help create situations in which the brain finds it natural to give those correct instructions. Training routines are designed to isolate the different functions of binocular vision and work on those that

---

CHOOSING AN EYE DOCTOR

The categories of eye practitioners can be confusing. Optometrists, who are graduates of a four-year postcollege professional school of optometry, are primary health-care providers who prescribe glasses and examine the eyes for disease. In most states, optometrists are also licensed to treat certain types of disease. Ophthalmologists, who belong to a medical specialty, are trained to treat disease and perform surgery; they may or may not prescribe glasses. Opticians make the glasses prescribed by others. The term "oculist," once applied to both optometrists and ophthalmologists, is no longer used.

Vision therapy is a form of neurophysiological treatment for disorders or dysfunctions, not disease. Today most eye doctors who offer vision therapy are optometrists certified by the College of Optometrists in Vision Development.

To find an eye doctor who offers vision therapy, ask your family eye doctor to refer you or call Binocular Vision Associates in Elkins Park or King of Prussia, Pennsylvania, at the toll-free vision hotline, 1-800-245-2773.

need help. They typically consist of doing familiar tasks under unfamiliar conditions. The patient will read, or draw, or follow a moving object with his eyes. He may do so while looking through Polaroid glasses that separate the sight in the two eyes so that the brain cannot rely on one eye alone but must practice its use of the other, or through a prism that stimulates his ability to move his eyes in and out in tandem, or through lenses that alternately stimulate and relax the focusing system. With enough practice, the brain learns to send the right instructions to the eyes without the help of the therapist's devices. Once a person reaches this point, the cure usually is lasting, for then the habit of doing it right is reinforced during every waking moment; it becomes easier and more comfortable to do it right. It is not like a workout that must be repeated daily to keep the muscles in shape.

Other kinds of visual and vision-related skills can be improved with vision therapy. Skills such as peripheral vision and visual reaction time—essential in driving and many sports—can readily be developed with practice on therapeutic instruments. So can perceptual skills which are often undeveloped in children who experience learning difficulties in the early years of school. Examples are eye-hand coordination, visual memory, and figure-ground perception, which is the ability to separate the essential from the irrelevant in what one sees.

For some, "vision therapy" may call up the image of eye exercises, with the implication that it somehow strengthens our eyes. The idea of exercise is misleading. (Today's vision therapy should not be confused with the routines prescribed by the "Bates method" that was popular several decades ago.) The muscles of our eyes are anywhere from fifty to one hundred times as strong as they need to be to do the work we ask of them: we need no visual push-ups. What happens might better be compared to learning to touch-type or play the piano or ride a bicycle: it is not the strength of the muscles that matters but what we do with them, or, better, what we tell them to do. Learning those skills consists, like vision therapy, in teaching the brain to send the right messages to the body. It takes practice but not muscular development.

As one might suppose, the likely duration and chance of success in vision therapy depend mainly on the nature of the problem and the

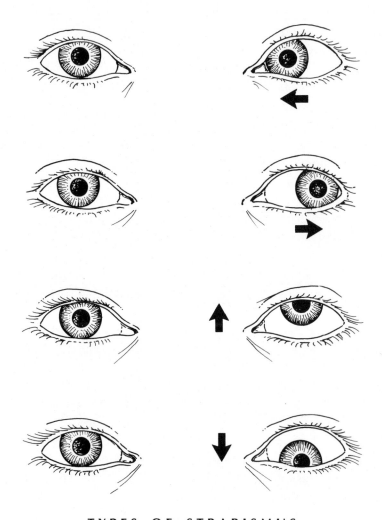

TYPES OF STRABISMUS

state of the patient. A young, healthy, motivated person with a disorder that is not too severe has better than nine chances in ten of a quick, complete, and lasting cure. Change any of these circumstances for the worse, and the odds are likely to be less favorable. Not always, however: vision therapy is more than 90 percent successful in treating the most common visual disorder of older people. In general, a course of vision therapy typically involves an hour or two a week and seldom lasts less than three months or more than nine.

Success can be measured in two ways. One is by the patient himself: Is he performing better and feeling better? Did he get what he came for? Those questions are of course best answered by the patient. But the eye doctor can also measure his work, or, for that matter, the work of another therapist, with clinical accuracy. Each of the various visual skills can be measured before and after treatment with diagnostic tests that yield objective results. As one would expect, the results of these tests usually jibe with the patients' own evaluations. The tests' importance lies in the fact that they provide corroborating evidence that is lacking in such other forms of treatment as psychotherapy. (A great deal of research has demonstrated the efficacy of vision therapy with such objective measures. See Appendix B for a summary of research findings.)

Until recently, throwing away one's glasses was not a goal of vision therapy. We developmental optometrists accepted refractive error—near- and farsightedness and astigmatism—as givens that would still be there after the most successful treatment. The patient who came in wearing glasses would usually walk out wearing them after his therapy, though the prescription might be less strong. If we were successful, he would be using his vision much more comfortably and effectively; he would be seeing better, but through the same glasses.

Today that is changing. A new form of treatment that uses the principle of biofeedback has succeeded in reducing and sometimes eliminating some forms of nearsightedness. This new myopia-control treatment, which we describe in detail in Chapter 10, now makes it possible for many adults indeed to throw away their glasses, for some others to put off the need for bifocals, and for some children to prevent the onset of myopia and thus never wear the glasses they would otherwise have needed.

In the chapters that follow, we will describe the role that vision therapy plays in people's lives from childhood to retirement, and in activities as diverse as working at a video display terminal, rehabilitating juvenile delinquents, driving more safely, engaging in athletics—and more. We begin at the beginning of life.

3

HOW VISION DEVELOPS

THE PRESCHOOL YEARS

We start life with the potential for vision, but vision itself we must acquire through our own efforts, and how well we succeed in those efforts goes a long way toward determining how well we will function in our world.

In the words of Arnold Gesell, the physician who was the great pioneer in the study of children's vision, a child is "born with a pair of eyes, but not with a visual world. He must build that world himself, and it is his private creation. . . .The space world thus becomes part of him. To no small degree, he is it."

In humans the development of vision is relatively slow. A chick has vision virtually from the moment of birth; on its first day after hatching, it shows by successfully pecking its food that it can coordinate eye and bill. For us, by contrast, it takes about ten years, often more, for the visual system to achieve complete development.

Vision develops not by itself but in intimate relation with the growth of our other abilities—our use of our bodies and our minds. Each stage of physical and mental development has its visual aspect, and understanding that visual aspect is essential to understanding the child's growth. The development of vision, however, is far less conspicuous than the stages of other kinds of growth. We can easily observe a child learning to crawl, to walk, to talk, but we cannot as easily see the subtle visual learning that accompanies and makes possible each of those advances. We can tell at a glance that a five-year-old is not fully grown; but that glance does not tell us if his visual system is ready for the demands of school.

It should be obvious that this understanding of the role of vision has crucial implications for the care of children. Regrettably, those implications have not been acted upon. Although our current understanding dates back to the late 1940s, when Gesell began publishing his work, the pediatric community—the various professions that deal with children—has yet to incorporate this essential knowledge into its daily practices. Children are penalized every day by practitioners who fail to grasp the role of vision in the growth of those entrusted to their care. In our opinion, there is no excuse for this. The information has been available for four decades and is neither difficult to understand nor expensive to practice.

The world of a newborn is very small, and so too is his visual world. He cannot effectively see further than about 8 inches—the distance to his mother's face when she is holding him—and he cannot coordinate his eyes. He usually appears to be staring rather than looking. Most of his perception comes through the senses of touch and taste and hearing.

What happens starting at birth can best be described as a reaching out to grasp the world, first with the hands, then with the eyes, which extend the child's grasp beyond the reach of the arms and of the other senses. As his visual grasp increases, he will come to rely more and more on his vision for information. It is an active process in which the developing child uses his vision to capture and understand the world in which he must function if he is to survive. It is not a smooth advance but one of jumps forward followed by periods of seeming regression during which the child is digesting and mastering the space he has just added to his private visual world. That world is what Richard S. Kavner, in his excellent book *Your Child's Vision*, calls the child's "personal space."

By the time he is six months old, the infant has begun to coordinate his eyes with his arm movements. He is more able to shift his attention, a necessary forerunner to eye-hand coordination. He focuses better on objects close to him, and he has begun the long process of developing binocular vision: the use of the eyes as a team that enables us to understand and measure space. As yet, however, he has very little depth perception. His personal space now extends out about 2 feet. (These distances and times are all approximate. Many children will go somewhat faster or slower, and there is no cause for alarm unless the child falls far behind the norm.)

By eight to twelve months the child has extended his personal space out to 3 feet, well beyond the reach of his hands. His eyes focus well in that near space, and he now notices objects in a mid-range of 3 to 10 feet. He can recognize his mother's face. This is a complex achievement of the infant's vision and brain. It means that he has begun to have visual memory: the ability to store an image in his mind. He can scan an object—his mother's face, for example—with his eyes, separating out the details he wants from all the other information his eyes are sending him; he can then compare the resulting shape with the image in his memory and conclude that the pictures match: what he sees is his mother.

In his second year the child must learn to use vision in correlation with his rapidly expanding bodily abilities: he needs vision to help him walk and talk. As he learns to talk, the child is making another complex advance in the use of vision and mind. He is integrating vision and language, the thing seen with its spoken symbol. This skill will be the bedrock of the academic learning that will occupy him during many of the years to come. It is as necessary to the survival of a modern child as the ability to track game was to his hunter ancestors.

By the time he is two years old one can observe that the child's eyes are beginning to lead his actions. Vision, the sense with the longest reach, the only sense that can scan, is starting to take over as his primary tool of perception; the child is reliving in a few months the shift in dominance from the other senses to vision that took our remote ancestors millions of years. Now he can turn head and eyes without turning his body. He can see another person's eyes at 5 to 8 feet. His binocular vision extends to 2 or 3 feet, though it is far from perfect even in that space. The absence of binocular vision is not always easy to discern. At times the eyes visibly drift apart, but at other times the child's eyes may be moving as a team and appear to be focusing on the object that interests him, while the brain may not yet have achieved the ability to fuse the two images and so be able to see space in its three dimensions.

Also around two, he achieves still another complex advance. He begins—just begins—to learn to visualize a hypothetical action. He begins to see in his mind's eye what would happen if he were to put this object in that place—this toy off the edge of the table—instead of having to find out only by trial and error as he did before. He is beginning to understand cause and effect: another way in which vision and mind develop in tandem. He has also learned by now that the world is a permanent place. The visual aspect of this is that he no longer believes, as he once did, that the world disappears when he covers his eyes. Before, when it was his turn to hide in a game of hide-and-seek, he covered his eyes in the belief that the world then disappeared; now he knows that the world doesn't work that way. Also he is doing better at coordinating his senses: turning his head, for example, to see what he has just heard.

By about halfway through his third year the child shows some verbal understanding of the space he is mastering with his vision: he grasps the concepts behind such words as "near" and "far," "up" and "down," "on" and "under." His visual world is precarious, and he is still largely dependent on manual contact: if he loses touch of an object, he is likely to lose sight of it also. Though he is binocular in his near area, he cannot always coordinate his eyes, and one or the other may be seen to drift.

Three is a relatively stable time. His eye-hand movements are advanced enough so that, while drawing or painting, he can keep the lines within the bounds of the paper. He can scan without moving his head—this will be very important later on—and he can use his hands for one task while he directs his eyes elsewhere. Within his personal space, which now extends out to 7 to 10 feet, he is fully binocular.

At about three and a half the child typically experiences a period of confusion during which he seems to regress. He shows by stuttering or stumbling or just fatigue that the new coordination between his visual and motor systems is still immature. His hold on his visual world is uncertain because he is exploring space in new ways, and so his eye-hand movements and binocular vision may seem to work less well than they did earlier.

Four is once again a stable period. The child can maintain eye contact and concentrated visual attention out to 10 to 16 feet, not far from the distance he will need to have mastered when he goes to school a year later. He can coordinate body and vision to catch and throw a ball, and follow it with his eyes in flight, and he can run smoothly at changing speeds.

Parents will of course want to provide the best conditions for their child's visual development. Along with the general principles of child-rearing, two points are of particular importance.

The child's vision needs stimulation. Since, as we have seen, visual growth is a constant reaching out, it is important to provide the child with interesting things to look at that will draw his attention beyond the present range of his vision. It is equally important not to constrict his field of vision so that there is no reason for him to try to expand its reach. An example is the playpen, in which vision is pretty much limited to a couple of feet. Leaving a child too often for too many hours in the playpen can discourage his visual growth; indeed, the less time spent there, the better. Being outdoors has the opposite effect. Indoors a child's visual field is limited by the four walls of the room; outside, he can try to gaze off as far as the horizon. "Go out and get some fresh air," parents will say. They might also say, at least to themselves: "Go outside and stretch your vision."

Nutrition is critical to vision: the eyes and the brain, which make up less than 2 percent of our bodily weight, eat up one-quarter of our nourishment. Again, the general principles of a good diet apply, and some aspects are particularly relevant to the eyes. A diet plentiful in vegetables and fresh fruits and the B vitamins is good for developing vision. On the negative side, recent research has shown that deficiencies in calcium and chromium—which can be caused by too much refined carbohydrate and sugar in the diet—are associated with near-sightedness. A shortage of those chemicals weakens the structure of the eye and leaves it vulnerable to the stretching under the pressure of close work that results in myopia.

Parents will want to watch for any symptoms of an emerging visual disorder in a preschool child. In later life, myopia is of course by far the most common of such disorders. If the child goes on to higher education and a career involving close-to-the-eyes work, as most people do nowadays, then the odds of being nearsighted are better than fifty-fifty. However, the great majority of people become nearsighted during their school years. Only a very small number of children, 1 or

NUTRITION FOR CHILDREN'S VISION

Good diet and an ample supply of the necessary vitamins are essential to the development of a child's vision. Here are guidelines for the adequate daily supply of nutrients, and signs of deficiency that may appear in the eyes. (See p. 171 for more on nutrition and vision.)

PROTEIN: Two grams daily for every 2.2 pounds of body weight. Poor vision is one sign of possible protein deficiency.

CARBOHYDRATES: One gram for every pound of body weight. Cloudiness of the eyes is a sign of deficiency.

HYDROCARBONS (oils and fats): About one-fourth of a child's calories should be in hydrocarbons.

VITAMIN A

from birth to six months	1,500 international units (IU)
six months to one year	2,000 international units (IU)
one year to four years	5,000 international units (IU)
four years to ten years	15,000 international units (IU)

Avoid overdoses of vitamin A, which can be harmful. Signs of deficiency include difficulty adjusting to darkness and changing intensities of light, a dry lusterless appearance of the cornea and surface of the eyeball, sties, burning or inflamed or itching eyes.

VITAMIN B_1

from birth to six months	0.5 milligram
six months to four years	0.7 milligram
four years to ten years	2.0 milligrams

Signs of deficiency include unclear vision, inflammation of internal eye tissues or ocular nerves, dry, burning sensation in the eye, double vision, weakening of the ocular muscles, involuntary oscillation of the eyeball (nystagmus).

VITAMIN B_2

from birth to six months	0.6 milligram
six months to four years	0.8 milligram
four years to ten years	2.0 milligrams

Signs of deficiency include appearance of blood vessels in the cornea, cloudiness of the eyes, cataracts, burning or itching eyes, sensitivity to light and excessive tearing, reduced acuity, gritty sensation in the eyelids.

VITAMIN B₃

from birth to six months	8 milligrams
six months to one year	9 milligrams
one year to four years	10 milligrams
four years to ten years	20 milligrams

PANTOTHENIC ACID

from birth to one year	5 milligrams
one year to ten years	10 milligrams

VITAMIN B₆

from birth to four years	0.7 milligram
four years to ten years	2.0 milligrams

Signs of deficiency include conjunctivitis (pinkeye), flaky dermatitis around eyes and eyebrows.

VITAMIN B₁₂

from birth to four years	3 micrograms
four to ten years	5 micrograms

Signs of deficiency include trouble focusing, blocking of central vision (scotoma).

VITAMIN C

from birth to one year	40 milligrams
one year to four years	50 milligrams
four years to ten years	60 milligrams

Signs of deficiency include sudden appearance of bulging of the eyes (exophthalmos).

VITAMIN D

400 international units at all ages.
Avoid excessive doses, especially for children with heart disease.

VITAMIN E

from birth to four years	10 international units
four years to ten years	30 international units

CALCIUM

from birth to one year	600 milligrams
one year to four years	800 milligrams
four years to ten years	1,000 milligrams

Signs of deficiency include increasing myopia.

CHROMIUM

from birth to one year	10 micrograms
one year to four years	60 micrograms
four years to ten years	80 micrograms

Signs of deficiency include focusing problems and myopia.

ZINC

from birth to one year	5 milligrams
one year to four years	10 milligrams
four years to ten years	15 milligrams

IRON
18 milligrams for all ages.

Table adapted from Richard S. Kavner, *Your Child's Vision* (New York: Simon & Schuster, 1985).

---

2 percent, are born myopic, and usually such children are severely afflicted. Prompt action is essential in these cases. It might seem that the problem could wait till the child goes to school, but that is a risky course to follow. A very nearsighted child cannot see well enough to reach out with his eyes. He will be handicapped in the progressive visual growth we have described, a handicap that will do him lasting damage. Fortunately, there is no need to wait. A one-year-old can be fitted with glasses, and contact lenses are feasible even before that.

Parents who observe symptoms of nearsightedness should seek immediate help. Habitual squinting is the surest sign of nearsightedness

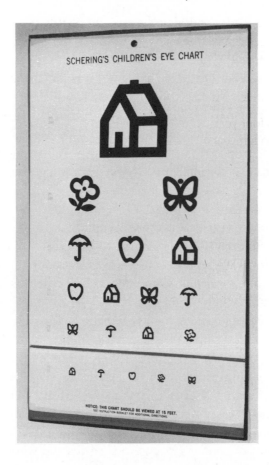

EYE CHART FOR PRESCHOOL CHILDREN

Reproduced by permission from Harold S. Stein, and Bernard J. Slatt and Raymond M. Stein: *The Ophthalmic Assistant*, 5th ed. (St. Louis: C. V. Mosby, 1988)

—indeed, the literal meaning of "myopia" is "shut eye." The myopic child tends to be passive, to avoid much physical activity, to shun risk. Because his visual reach is limited, he lives in a constricted world. He prefers close-up sedentary activities and he gets very close to what he is doing. He buries his nose in a book. Such a child was Michael B.

•

MICHAEL was just two when his parents began to notice that something was wrong with his sight. Until then this unusually bright child had concealed his exceptionally poor sight. He rarely wanted to watch television, "even 'Sesame Street,' " his mother said, and when he did he would put his face almost up against the screen. One day the family was looking at prints of a roll of pictures. Michael brought each picture right up against his eyes. The parents decided they had to seek help. Two ophthalmologists who examined him said he was severely near-sighted and proposed only to fit him with full-strength glasses. Dissatisfied, the parents came to us at the suggestion of one of our patients.

Michael was about two and a half when he started treatment with us. He was indeed severely myopic, one of that small percentage of children born very nearsighted. His blurred sight, we were certain, was going to cause him to miss out on the normal development of binocular vision. We believed he was headed for serious trouble when he got to school.

We started Michael with glasses that provided a less-than-full correction: very myopic people often cannot take full correction at first, but must work up to it in stages. The partial correction would enable him to see well enough to develop his vision but would also keep his eyes trying to see better. We gradually increased his prescription—though never to full correction—so that by school age he would be able to see the blackboard. We changed him to contacts at age four so that he would not start school wearing glasses. He has used contacts since then.

We also started Michael at age four in vision therapy designed to help him develop both binocular vision and his perceptual skills. We aimed at improving his eye-hand coordination, his ability to distinguish objects visually, and his visual memory. Soon he would need those skills in school, and we wanted him to be ready. Michael took readily to the therapy, which lasted nine months. In this his parents were a great help. His mother said he felt when going to therapy that he was "going to school like his older sisters." The drawings he brought home went up on the refrigerator with the other children's schoolwork and were equally praised.

Still, willing though he has been, Michael has not had an easy time of it. At seven, he had to come back for more therapy when it was obvious that his depth perception was not developing normally.

At nine, Michael is doing very well in fourth grade. His mother reports that he is "an excellent student, in all the top groups." He is also an avid young athlete whose sports include some that are visually very demanding: he plays catcher in baseball, and plays tennis and basketball as well. (We have, however, asked his parents to keep him out of contact sports like football and even soccer, for fear of damage to his fragile retinas, which in the very myopic may be prone to detaching.) After school he likes to get out on his roller skates.

Although he is still very myopic, Michael's personality is not that of the shy, studious, nearsighted person. He is an exceptionally friendly, active, and outgoing child. His mother believes, as do we, that he would not have turned out this way had he started school wearing thick glasses and handicapped by poor visual skills.

It is important to note that, though he has made enormous gains, Michael B. is not yet out of the woods. At nine, he is entering the years in which so many people become progressively more nearsighted. But now, thanks to a new form of therapy that we describe in Chapter 10, there is an excellent chance that Michael can be kept from becoming any more nearsighted than he is today.

•

Strabismus, a turned eye, is the most obvious of visual problems in child or adult. Where other disorders can be observed only through their consequences, a turned eye is immediately noticeable. Usually the eye is turned in or out (cross- or walleyed), but sometimes it is up or down. Since at age three or four a child's visual system is still unstable, it is normal for an eye to drift in or out occasionally, and parents should not overreact to a passing phenomenon. But if the eye is persistently turned for days on end in the same direction, the child's vision should be examined, and if that examination confirms the presence of strabismus, it is important to take prompt action to prevent lasting damage.

Strabismus usually shows up between the ages of eighteen months and five years. It afflicts from 2 to 4 percent of the population. Each year about one million children show evidence of strabismus. Its causes are not fully understood. Sometimes a childhood illness such as chickenpox or an emotional trauma such as the death of a parent can produce strabismus by disrupting the ability of the two eyes to work together. The consequences of strabismus go beyond the aesthetic. The preschool years, as we have seen, are when the child's mind devotes itself to learning the difficult skill of binocular vision. If one eye is turned, binocular vision is impossible because the brain is getting different images from the two eyes. Finding this intolerable, the brain simply rejects the messages sent by the turned eye and in effect sees with the one straight eye. In time the ability to see in the turned eye fades with disuse and may disappear permanently. Strabismus in those early years may prevent the essential learning of binocular vision even if the affliction eventually disappears or is successfully treated later on. This is because the brain tends to learn visual skills at the usual time or not at all. So in later years the growing child's mind will direct its attention elsewhere even if it has not mastered binocular vision.

Parents of a child with strabismus face three choices: doing nothing, surgery, and vision therapy. (There is also a form of treatment using drugs that is seldom practiced today.)

Doing nothing is often advocated on the grounds that the child may outgrow his strabismus and his turned eye will right itself without intervention. In our opinion this is a dangerous route to follow. It is quite true that the child may outgrow the visible cosmetic problem in the sense that his eyes will appear to be correctly aligned. But if he has missed the time for learning binocular vision, those two eyes will not actually be working together and he will not perceive space in depth. And that is a severe handicap. He may also miss out on other forms of learning that depend on good visual development.

The same hazard applies to surgery. Surgeons will attempt to re-align the eye by changing the balance of the eye muscles (though in many cases the eye muscles are in fact not imbalanced). This surgery may correct the cosmetic problem, but, as in the case of doing nothing, the child may be left without binocular vision. Often surgery does not correct even the cosmetic problem. The eye remains turned, or, sometimes after an interval of months or years, the eye will turn in a different direction. Nothing has been solved and the eye's capacity for recovery has been permanently weakened. The chance of success in surgical treatment of strabismus is about 20 percent—dismal odds for an action whose consequences are irreversible. All too often, Emile Javal's description of such surgery as "the massacre of the ocular muscles" is as valid today as when this first practitioner of vision therapy wrote it a century and a half ago.

Vision therapy is the parents' third option. Unlike surgery, it has no irreversible consequences; if it fails to cure the strabismus, no damage has been done to the child's eye. Most of the time, however, vision therapy does not fail. Its success rate is about 75 percent, almost four times that of surgery. Early treatment, again, is important to increase the chances for natural learning of binocular vision and to head off the possible side effects of failure in the child's first experiences in school.

•

JESSICA K. was four and a half when her parents began to notice something was wrong. Her right eye turned in and stayed that way, not like the wandering eye common in young children. She turned her head to look at people. She was unusually clumsy. Repeatedly she would trip over things she should have seen. She was falling down much too often. Worried about kindergarten, which Jessica was about to enter, her parents brought her to us. Jessica suffered from alternating strabismus: each eye would turn in separately from time to time. The brain finds it difficult to cope with the garbled messages sent by the eyes. When Jessica turned her head, it was to try to avoid seeing double. She was half a year behind in the development of her perceptual skills.

We started Jessica on a course of vision therapy, combined with home exercises, which lasted nine months. For the first three months we asked Jessica to wear an eye patch over her better left eye during therapy to help induce her turned right eye to work. She took to the therapy readily, both in our office and at home; according to her parents, "it was something of her own."

Jessica's therapy started just before her year in kindergarten.

At first she could not see the blackboard except from the front row and she had trouble drawing pictures and forming letters. By the end of the school year her scholastic problems had vanished. She could see the board, and her visual skills were up to normal. Her parents reported that she was "enthusiastic about reading."

In her perceptual skills Jessica had taken a remarkable leap forward, from half a year behind average to four years and eight months above average, all in nine months. Therapy had brought about this sudden great advance in two ways: first, it enabled her to use skills she already had; and second, it added to those skills. Jessica no longer fell down more than other children her age. She could now catch a playground ball, which she could not do earlier in the year.

Jessica K.'s once-turned eyes were now normal both in appearance and in function. The cosmetic problem was gone and so was the visual problem. Jessica's strabismus was completely cured—without surgery.

•

Perceptual problems usually manifest themselves in the child's motor skills because his eyes lead his physical actions; a mistaken lead causes a mistaken action. If the child is lagging in the growth of his motor skills and no pathology is present, it is likely to be because of a visual problem. Any such lag should flash a warning signal: this child may have a learning problem when he reaches school. If he is lagging in several skills, the possibility becomes a probability. Similarly, a child who has, say, worn an orthopedic brace is more likely to have a visual motor problem in school, because his motor impediment will have affected his visual learning as well.

Parents should watch for any difficulty the child may have in his successive motor milestones: sitting up, crawling, creeping, walking. Other symptoms to watch for are dragging one leg, putting shoes on the wrong foot, trouble learning to tie laces or button buttons, unusual clumsiness. A child with a perceptual-motor problem is likely to have trouble learning to skip, and on stairs (especially going down) may tend to go one step at a time. He may avoid doing puzzles.

Keep in mind that children must crawl before they can walk: they must pass through each of the motor milestones if their skills are to develop properly. Parents should not attempt to bypass a skill with which the child is having trouble, but rather help him master it. For many of the motor skills, there are games on the market that will enhance a child's opportunity to learn. The parents may also take the child to a developmental optometrist to see if there is a visual problem that can be treated.

•

LINDSAY G.'s parents observed when she was very young that something was wrong. Although she was a bright, alert child, she kept bumping into things. She complained frequently of headaches, and she was afraid to go to bed because of the shadows she thought she was seeing. Two eye practitioners found nothing wrong with Lindsay's sight, but a third, a specialist in vision therapy, diagnosed amblyopia, or lazy eye. Lindsay was getting virtually no information from her left eye—only those shadows—although there appeared to be nothing wrong with the eye itself. The cause in her case was what is called anisometropia: the sight in the two eyes is so different that the brain, unable even with glasses to reconcile the conflicting images it is receiving, suppresses the messages from one eye. Lindsay was extremely farsighted in one eye, hardly at all in the other.

The eye doctor prescribed a patch for her good right eye, which would force the lazy left eye to do its share of the work. Lindsay, who was then four, wore the patch for three months. The treatment was successful. Lindsay's headaches vanished and so did the frightening shadows. She went off to school and did well in the first three grades. She learned to read on schedule and did well in sports. In fourth grade the required reading increased the demands on her vision to the point where she once again needed therapy (see p. 67). But the patch had given her crucial help in the all-important first years of school—a high payoff for a simple form of therapy.

•

At about age five the child will enter school. Now for the first time he will have to keep pace with others, will have to perform to standards set not by his own rate of maturing but by the teacher and the other members of the group. A delay of six months in his visual development, which might otherwise be harmless, can have damaging effects in school if it impedes his performance. If he is failing in his first experience in this new environment, the child is likely to be soured on school and to turn against learning in general.

Just as his body is not fully grown, the child's visual system is still not fully developed. It will go on developing for another five years or longer, though the rate of change will slow down. But by age five the child's vision must have reached certain well-defined levels if he is to meet the expectations of school.

His most obvious need is for visual acuity in order to see what the teacher is doing at the front of the room. The Snellen wall chart with its big E and the expression of normal sight as 20/20 are based on the assumption that the child needs normal sight at 20 feet, which was taken to be the average distance to the blackboard. (20/20 means that one sees at 20 feet what the normal eye sees at that distance. 20/40 means that one sees at 20 feet what the normal eye sees at 40 feet. 20/ 10 means one sees at 20 feet what the normal eye sees at 10 feet.) Acuity as measured by the Snellen or a similar chart is a function of the size and shape of the eyeball, not a skill the child has learned, and any deficiency in acuity can only (with exceptions we will take up later) be remedied with glasses or contact lenses. Acuity is also the only aspect of a child's sight that is routinely examined when he starts school.

The child needs another set of visual skills, not measured by the Snellen chart, that differ from acuity in two essential ways: they are learned skills, and they involve movement. Any deficiency is due to a delay in learning, not to a flaw in the eyeball to be corrected by glasses. Though the child will continue to improve these skills for the next five years or more, he must have reached certain minimum levels by the time he starts school in order to cope with its demands. Since schools regrettably do not test entering students for these skills, parents may want to seek an eye doctor who will test their child. They should certainly do so if they have any reason to believe the child is lagging in his visual development.

Visual pursuit, or eye-tracking, is the ability to follow an object in motion with the eyes. The action is controlled by the six small muscles attached to the eyeball. Effective visual pursuit requires adequate muscles and learning how to direct them. When the skill is fully developed, usually not till about age seven, the eyes move smoothly in pursuit of the object, but at five their motion is still visibly jerky. This skill is essential to following what is going on in the classroom (and therefore to paying attention), to keeping one's place while reading, and to catching a ball. It is in the child's performance in those activities that deficiencies will become evident.

Fixation, the ability to bring both eyes to bear on the same object, must be well advanced. A child whose fixation is poor will have trouble in concentrating and keeping his attention on what is going on in class. Focusing, or accommodation, which is accomplished by a change in the shape of the lens, should also be well advanced. A child whose focusing is working poorly will be confused by detail—for example, when reading, by the difference between the words "these" and "those" or "hit" and "kit."

The small, rapid eye shifts known as saccadic (pronounced suh-CADD-ic) movements will become critically important later on when the child has to read for any length of time. At age five, before the child is reading, a saccadic deficiency may appear as a difficulty in shifting the eyes from one target to another.

The child's binocular vision must be well developed by the time he enters school. This is how he sees in three dimensions and thus is how he locates himself and others in space. A child with poor binocular vision will seem clumsy, and is likely to have trouble putting one block on top of another or pouring water into a cup—all because he cannot judge space accurately.

These visual skills typically work together, so that a lag in one will affect the results obtained by the others. Thus a child will use acuity of sight, along with eye-tracking and binocular vision, to understand what is happening at the front of the room, then, shifting his attention to what is immediately in front of him, will use saccadic movement and focusing to carry out the teacher's instructions.

These are skills of vision proper. There is another skill he will need that at first seems unrelated to vision. In order to pay attention to what is going on, he must be able to sit in a comfortable, balanced position. His sense of posture derives in part from messages his eyes send to his balancing mechanism. The child has been gradually developing his sense of posture as he learned first to crawl, then to walk, and then to run. A child whose posture is not yet ready for school will be fidgety and will have trouble paying attention.

What we have described is where a child should be in his visual development by the time he starts school. Of course many children are in fact not ready. One estimate based on a very large survey dating from the early 1950s is that two children in every ten enter school with vision that has not yet reached the stage they need for what they have to do. Our own experience has been that the rate nowadays is much higher, that about four children in ten are not visually ready when they start school. Recently kindergarten teachers have been reporting that a rising proportion of their entering classes are not ready for school. The number of teachers who make this observation also seems to be rising year by year.

"Why is there such an increased frequency of visual-motor problems in children today compared to twenty-five years ago?" We have heard that question time and again from veteran kindergarten teachers. We find two major changes in our culture that go a long way toward explaining why so many more children are not visually ready for school.

Children's games have changed radically in the last quarter-century. Such traditional games as jacks, stoopball, pickup sticks, marbles, hopscotch, and jumping rope are seldom seen today. Each of those games, and indeed virtually any traditional game, was a challenge in visual-motor coordination. Playing those games, therefore, was an important part of children's visual development. Today those games have been largely replaced by electronic and battery-operated toys and games whose manufacturers compete to reduce the demands on users for visual and motor effort. A lot of practice time has been lost.

Television, of course, occupies a large chunk of most children's waking hours. We have no intention of adding to the volumes that have been written on the influence of television on children, so we will confine ourselves to its effects on their visual development. We believe those effects are harmful whatever may be the content of the programs children are watching. Television is harmful because it is passive—one of the most passive of human experiences. It asks nothing of a child's visual system beyond a passive stare, and little if any more of his mind. When watching the tube he practices none of the visual skills he should be learning at that stage in his life. Nor does it call on his visual imagination. In this, television differs from radio, which otherwise is also a passive experience. Someone listening to a story on the radio must imagine in pictures the scenes that are being described in words. For a child, that is useful practice of a mental skill, the creation of visual images, which must be learned like the other aspects of vision.

If it is true that children watch an average of four hours of television a day, that is a huge loss of time which they might otherwise spend practicing their visual skills. Add to that the practice lost owing to modern children's games, and the learning time taken out of their lives becomes frighteningly large.

Children learn skills the same way everyone does, by practice, and nowadays they are losing a great deal of practice time. Is it any wonder that kindergarten teachers complain that so many children are unprepared? Or that so many children in the early grades need some form of remedial therapy to make up for the visual experiences they have never had?

4

READING AND VISION
IN SCHOOL

WHY SO MANY CHILDREN CAN'T
SEE TO READ

•

BRENDAN M. came to us in April of his second-grade year. He was eight years and eight months old, and an unusually bright child. But he was in serious trouble: he couldn't seem to learn to read. No one could figure out why. Brendan had gotten off to a good start in life, as the healthy child of parents who were both college graduates. He was a happy boy who loved his first school experience in a cooperative play group. It was in first grade that the first signs of trouble appeared. Despite his natural ability, he wasn't keeping up with his peers in learning to read. A perceptive nun who taught him commented: "I have a sense that Brendan doesn't see what I see. Are you sure he's seeing it right?" A standard eye examination showed him to be mildly farsighted, and thereafter he wore glasses for close work.

But by late in second grade Brendan had fallen far behind. His teacher reported that he was making no progress in reading and writing. He frequently reversed letters. He had "great difficulty with words on a page." In arithmetic, he could not tell when a number was written incorrectly, and he was beginning to reverse two-digit numbers. The teacher could see that Brendan was under stress. He would turn his paper sideways, push away his glasses, rub his eyes. He was becoming quarrelsome, and would lash out angrily if another child supplied the right answer. He had been seen by a reading tutor, but she reported that he was making no improvement at all. He was complaining of headaches and discomfort when trying to read or write.

The school psychologist was consulted. His tests showed Brendan to be of considerably above average intelligence, with an IQ of 131. Orally, in his use of words, he was far ahead of his age level. But his ability to concentrate and pay attention, though average, was below what his intellectual capacity suggested. He was eager to do what was expected of him but uncertain that he could meet the demands of school. "Incipient learning disability," the psychologist concluded.

At home, Brendan's parents saw his problems taking their toll on his personality. They watched helplessly as their son's once-cheery disposition turned sour. He was getting into frequent fights, and was frustrated and unhappy. "What's the matter with me?" he would say. Once he told his mother that when he tried to read "the words seem to melt on the page." Now his mother recalled that as a child she had had the same experience: "The words seemed to melt on the page." She wondered if Brendan had inherited some sort of visual problem from her.

•

Brendan's case is typical of a very large number of children. On any given day, there are millions like him in our schools, millions of children who just cannot manage reading. Four of them will be found in the average classroom of twenty-five. In the first two grades these children cannot learn to read, and in the later grades they cannot read to learn. They have been classed under various labels, such as "learning disabled," or most recently "attention-deficit disorder," all of which translate as: "We don't know why."

Indeed, no one knows why such a large number of otherwise normal children cannot manage reading. For they are normal in the sense that they are not lacking in intelligence. The many studies of "learning-disabled" children show them to be as intelligent on the average as their reading peers.

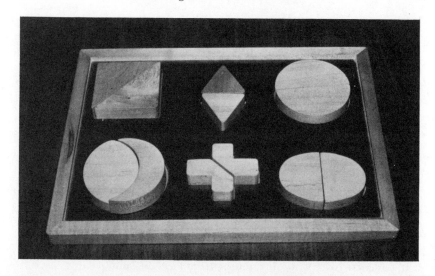

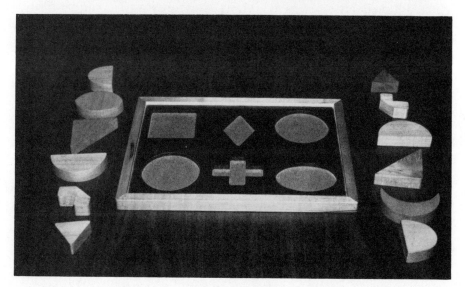

THE DIVIDED FORM BOARD

Shown here is a test that helps determine whether a child is visually ready to learn. The child is shown the assembled figures, each consisting of two pieces, then the figures are taken apart and the child is asked to put them together. This test determines whether the child has successfully made the transition from depending on touch for information to the reliance on vision that is necessary for success in school. The transition to visual dominance is usually achieved by the child's seventh year. A first-grade child should be able to complete this task in 90 seconds or less.

What happens to such children is sadly evident to those of us who spend a lot of time with the victims of reading problems. We know they started out to school happily at age five or six. They were eager to learn. Of course: they had been avid learners since the day of their birth, and natural curiosity is part of what defines us as human beings. Then such a child is confronted with reading. He cannot do it. He just cannot do it. He fails, and fails again and again. He is intellectually ready to learn, but the primary path to learning is through reading, and so his first experience of school, of the world of organized education, has become a disaster. He reacts as one does to failure. He gives up on learning. By age nine he hates school. He will become one of those hyperactive children who disrupt the classroom, or, at the other extreme, will withdraw silently into a corner. In time he may learn to read well enough to get by in school and, later, in life. But precious years have been irretrievably lost. He will perform below his potential, far below in many cases, and the damage to his personality and emotional well-being will be lifelong. The cost to him is high. So is the cost to society.

Why can't these children learn? We believe that visual disorders—disorders that can or might be remedied—are the culprit in a very large number of cases of learning disability. Statistics bear this out. One of us did a study that showed that almost three-quarters of reading-disabled children—73 percent, to be precise—suffered from a disorder of vision. This compares to 22 percent for children with no reading problem. Many other surveys over many years have produced similar results. (These studies are described in Appendix B.)

By now the evidence is overwhelming. Yet the importance of vision to learning disability is not generally recognized, and especially not where it matters most: in school. As one optometrist, Tole Greenstein, put it: "One of the better kept secrets of our time is the devastating effect that a visual problem has on an individual's ability to learn." Those who deny that vision plays a major role in learning problems rely on the evidence of the standard eye examination. This measures "refractive error"—the familiar near- and farsightedness and astigmatism, all of which are due to distortions in the shape of the eyeball. That, plus in many cases checking for disease or a turned eye, is all that shows up on the standard exam.

There is indeed no greater rate of learning disability among children with refractive error. In the case of myopia, the opposite is true. Nearsighted children tend to be better readers: the conventional image of the bespectacled bookworm finds confirmation in the statistics. From our point of view, that makes good sense. We believe most cases of myopia are the result of the eyeball adapting to the stress of prolonged near-point work. Good readers read more, and in so doing they are more likely to become nearsighted.

The eye screening given most children in most schools is unbelievably poor—so poor that it reveals less than 5 percent of visual problems. (If an X ray or blood test showed so little of what it is supposed to show, it would surely be unacceptable.) Once a year, or more often every two years, the school nurse sits the child 20 feet away from the familiar Snellen chart and measures his acuity at distance. And that's all. She does not test for learned visual skills (though a simple screening device could easily be designed for her use). Most of the time she does not even test the child's near acuity, although that of course is what he needs when reading. It seems incredible yet it is true that in a nation afflicted with reading problems our schools do not routinely find out if children can even see the page in front of them! It seems incredible yet it is true that far fewer schools have vision consultants than have dental consultants—as if we learned to read with our teeth, not our eyes!

The visual disorders found in so many learning-disabled children are those that have their causes beyond the retina, in their vision and visual perception. As we saw in the previous chapter, children start school before they have fully learned to use these systems. They are lacking in the background of experience on which perception is based and so are not yet fully able to interpret the evidence of their senses. Nor are their thinking processes mature. According to Jean Piaget, the great Swiss student of child development, all children must pass through stages of mental development in which their ways of thinking are distinctively different from those of adults. Only after they are about eleven do children begin to reason as adults do—and, unfortunately, a great many never make that last transition. Indeed, 30 percent of children have yet to make the transition when they reach fourteen, which means they enter high school without the capacity for adult reasoning that high school requires.

Before they reach the adult stage, children perceive the world dif-

TWO KINDS OF VISION PROBLEMS

Vision problems in school-age children fall into two broad categories besides the refractive errors treated by standard eye doctors.

One category consists of physiological disorders of vision proper, problems in how the eyes function as directed by the brain:

BINOCULAR FUSION: The ability to bring the two eyes together so that their images fuse and integrate and to maintain that fusion comfortably for sustained periods of time while, for example, reading or working on a computer terminal.

FOCUS (ACCOMMODATION): The ability to see clearly at a fixed distance and to shift focus quickly and with instantaneous clarity from one distance to another, as, for example, from desk to blackboard.

FIXATION: The ability to locate a target and stabilize the eyes so that their images of that target fall on the retina at the most desirable angle.

EYE MOVEMENTS: The ability to move the eyes quickly, accurately, and in precise coordination, as in, for example, reading or following a moving ball.

The second category consists of problems in visual perception, in how the child uses the information from the eyes:

VISUAL-VERBAL MATCH: The ability to match information from hearing, the spoken word, with that from vision, the written word, as one does in learning to read.

FIGURE-GROUND PERCEPTION: The ability to separate out what matters at the moment from surrounding information, as, for example, in concentrating on one problem among many on an arithmetic worksheet.

DIRECTIONALITY IN SPACE: The ability to tell up from down or left from right, as, for example, in seeing the difference between b and d, or "was" and "saw."

VISUAL FORM PERCEPTION: The ability to recognize differences in shape, as, for example, the shapes of letters.

VISUAL-MOTOR COORDINATION: The ability to coordinate vision and body actions, as, for example, eyes and hand in writing or catching a ball.

VISUAL IMAGERY: The ability to picture something that is not physically visible at the moment, as, for example, in scanning a word in the mind's eye to see if it looks properly spelled.

ferently. They are not miniature adults. They interpret evidence according to different mental standards that proceed in predictable patterns. Up to about seven, for example, children tend to believe anything they see. They are an excellent audience for a magician: they believe the rabbit really came out of the hat because that is what they saw and they have not yet learned to interpret the evidence of their eyes. Another example involves the principle of conservation. Pour a given amount of water from a tall, narrow beaker into one that is short and broad, in the presence of a five-year-old child. The five-year-old will invariably pick one beaker or the other as containing or having contained more water. Or press a piece of putty into various shapes. Again, the child will pick one shape as larger than others. Only later, again around seven, will his thinking develop so that he can perceive that different shapes can contain (or "conserve") the same quantity. Nor have many children yet established vision as their dominant sense, the sense on which they primarily rely for information. They still need to touch an object to grasp its reality—an obvious handicap in the classroom, where they must understand actions that take place beyond their arms' length.

Most children, as we well know, learn to read nonetheless. But a substantial minority are just not ready for what is a difficult undertaking in the best of circumstances. Dr. Arnold Gesell, whose child development clinic at Yale did the great pioneering work on the vision of children, estimated that from a quarter to a half of them are not "visually ready" when they enter first grade. These children will observe less, remember less, learn less, and in general be less efficient at what they do. Again, many of them will overcome the handicap and learn to read. But for many others the gap is too great. They will join the unhappy ranks of the learning-disabled. Their visual problems remain unnoticed, and indeed, they often do better than average on the Snellen chart. As Dr. William M. Ludlam, director of a learning-disability clinic, observed: "They'd make great buffalo hunters. But not good students."

The problems we developmental optometrists find in such children fall into two broad categories, with a bundle of related problems within each category. (See box on p. 50.) One group consists of physiological disorders of vision proper: the child cannot move his eyes well, or cannot focus quickly and accurately, or cannot use his eyes as a team for binocular vision. In the other category are disorders of perception which manifest themselves in what the child can or cannot do with his vision. An obvious example is poor eye-hand coordination that prevents him from forming letters with a pencil, spelling, or putting his thoughts down on paper. Another is the inability to connect in his mind what he sees with what he hears, so that he cannot carry out on paper the teacher's spoken instructions. Still another has to do with what is called "directionality"—the ability to tell left from right. This child cannot tell *b* from *d*, or *p* from *q* (the only difference between each pair of letters being in their left-right orientation), nor can he understand what is intended when he is told to move his eyes and hand from left to right across the page. Some children may show a surprising awareness that what they perceive is not what is out there. One child, told to copy figures in a drawing, asked: "Do you want me to copy them the way I see them or the way they really are?"

Although children typically show problems in both areas, the emphasis shifts with the changing requirements of school. In the first two grades, disorders of perception are usually more important to the child as a handicap to learning. Such a child was Marygrace K.

•

MARYGRACE K. was an attractive girl, five years and nine months old. She was three weeks into first grade at a Catholic academy where she had attended kindergarten. She was of average intelligence—tests showed an IQ of 100. But she had done poorly in kindergarten and was doing badly in first grade. Now it seemed likely that she would be sent back to repeat kindergarten.

Her teacher described Marygrace as a hyperactive child with a short attention span. Her mother said she was clumsy. When she came to us this child already seemed to be marked by failure. She looked down instead of looking people in the eye. She did not smile much.

Our examination showed Marygrace to be far behind in the development of her perceptual skills. Her ability to copy what she saw was about eighteen months behind her age—a potentially disastrous lag at that time of life. So was her ability to recognize and record digits flashed on a screen by an instrument

MARYGRACE'S WORK

Above are Marygrace's scores in a test of her ability to absorb and reproduce visual information. An instrument called the tachistoscope flashes on a screen groups of numbers which the patient tries to reproduce from memory. The first column shows Marygrace's score when the instrument displayed groups of three digits, showing each group for one-tenth of a second. In this test, before her therapy, she got 17 of 30 correct. The second column shows the result when the tachistoscope showed her groups of four digits for one-hundredth of a second each. In this more difficult test, after therapy, Marygrace got 40 of 40 correct. Note also the great improvement in her handwriting in only eight months.

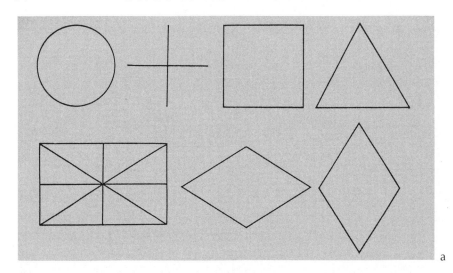

a

b

Above are Marygrace's drawings in what is called the Winter Haven Visual
Copy Forms Test. The patient is shown the whole group of geometrical figures (a), then is shown the individual figures one by one and asked to copy
them. This process tests the patient's eye-hand coordination and his or her
ability to organize and use spatial information. In the first two tests, before
(b) and during (c) therapy, Marygrace's performance is below average for her
age. In the last test (d) her skills have advanced in age level by 24 months—
in only 9 months' time.

c

d

called a tachistoscope. She had virtually no understanding of left and right; she could not follow an instruction to move an arm or leg on one or the other side. She could not bounce a ball with one hand, then the other, which is unusual at that age. Tests for other perceptual skills all showed her performing considerably below her age and intelligence levels.

We started Marygrace on a program of treatment that was to last ten months. The therapy provided her with concentrated practice in all the skills in which she was deficient. Believing it essential to offer her success rather than still more failure, we began by reinforcing and perfecting those skills which she could to some degree handle. Then, as soon as possible, but always building on success, we moved her on to gradually more advanced skills.

Marygrace's treatment was successful. Far from being put back, she performed exceedingly well in first grade; she was one of the best students. She went on to do equally well in second grade. When she was tested at the beginning of second grade—ten months after we first examined her—the difference was dramatic. Over the full range of perceptual skills, Marygrace tested in most cases above, and in some far above, the average for her age; in no case did she test below average. She now had no trouble with left and right and she could bounce that ball. Her scholastic achievement scores were on a third-grade level. In less than twelve months she had advanced by at least two years. Marygrace was doing well in school and, moreover, she seemed like a different child. Now she smiled and looked us in the eye. Her manner was self-assured. She even seemed more concerned about her personal appearance.

•

Would Marygrace have caught up to her class anyway, without our therapy? Unfortunately, the experience of many other children shows that the mere passage of time does not guarantee that the child will gain the skills she is lacking: the right kind of experience is also necessary. In any event the question in practice does not arise. In a perfect world, children like Marygrace would not be asked to read until they were visually ready. As we all know, however, our world is not perfect. In our world, school is a large-scale institution in which children must keep up with the group. The group will not wait for the Marygraces of our world. When she falls behind she will be branded a failure, in her own eyes as well as those of others.

DOES YOUR CHILD NEED HELP WITH VISUAL SKILLS? A Checklist for Parents

What follow are two lists of questions for parents of school-age children.

The first list of questions is about urgent signs of possible visual problems. If the answer to any one of these eleven questions is yes, the child should get a full evaluation of visual skills.

1. Does your child see double?
2. Does he get frequent headaches?
3. Does he have a short attention span while reading?
4. Does he while reading frequently lose his place or use a finger as a pointer?
5. Is he in the lowest reading group?
6. Does he have very poor handwriting?
7. Does he avoid reading?
8. Does he say that the print in a book is blurred or that it blurs in and out of focus?
9. Does he have difficulty seeing the chalkboard in school?
10. Does he make frequent reversals, such as "was" for "saw" or 34 for 43?
11. Does one of your child's eyes turn in or out?

This second list of questions is about less severe signs of troubled vision. If the answer to five or more of these questions is yes, the child's visual skills should be evaluated.

1. Does your child hold the book very close to the eyes (7 or 8 inches) while reading or writing?
2. Does he have his head turned while working at a desk?
3. Does he rest his head on his arm while reading or writing?
4. Does he cover one eye while reading?

5. Does he squint while doing close visual work?
6. Does he consistently show poor posture while doing close work?
7. Does he while reading move his head back and forth instead of just his eyes?
8. Does his reading homework take him longer than it should?
9. Does he report that print becomes blurry after prolonged reading, though at first it was clear?
10. Does he complain of words or letters running together?
11. Does he rub his eyes or blink excessively during or after close work?
12. Do his eyes appear red during or after reading?
13. Does he lose his place when moving his gaze from desk to chalkboard or when copying from text to notebook?
14. Does his writing slant up or down on the page, or is the spacing irregular between words or letters?
15. Does your child repeatedly omit or add or substitute small words while reading or writing?
16. Does he reread or skip words or lines without knowing he is doing it?
17. Does he fail to recognize the same word in the next sentence?
18. Does his reading comprehension decrease the longer he reads?
19. Does he have trouble sustaining concentration on any desk work?
20. Does he misalign the digits in columns of numbers?
21. Is he slow at copying?
22. Does he seem unable to stay on ruled lines when writing?
23. Does he turn or rotate the paper in order to draw lines in different directions?
24. Does he consistently have trouble putting thoughts on paper (for example, writing a letter describing a vacation trip)?
25. Does he have difficulty catching or hitting a ball?
26. Does he have difficulty closing buttons or tying shoelaces?
27. Does he have difficulty distinguishing left from right?
28. Does he get carsick?

A couple of years of repeated failure will do considerable damage to such a child. Even if she does catch up in her perceptual skills, she may never catch up academically, because her appetite for learning has been stunted and in the effort to get by in school she has formed bad scholastic habits that will outlast their cause. The same is true of children whose superior natural ability enables them to keep up despite a lag in their perceptual development. They will keep up but they will not work up to their potential: a child of 130 IQ, let us say, will do average work when he could do far better. We believe that in both cases the cost in lost potential and human unhappiness of waiting for nature to do it—which will probably never happen—is far too great when another way is available.

Unfortunately, children with perceptual problems seldom are brought to us as early as they should be. The issue is not as clear as it is when the child has an obviously visual problem. Usually other professionals are already involved, for, when a child with apparently good eyesight can't seem to learn, one is not likely to turn first to an optometrist. It is true that sometimes we succeed in removing the perceptual problem and the child still does not learn. Children who master the perceptual skills but still do not learn are suffering from some other impediment that must be resolved, if indeed it can be, by someone in another field—though it may still have been necessary first to remove the perceptual problem.

●

When we examined BRENDAN M., we found that he was suffering from several related disorders of vision. His complaints of headaches when he tried to read or write were understandable. Brendan literally couldn't read: any sustained close work was painful for his eyes. He was mildly farsighted, but that was corrected by his glasses. With or without glasses, however, he could not make his eyes work as a team—he could not make the two pictures his eyes saw fuse into a single stable image, and his binocular vision was poor. He could not hold his eyes in focus; that was why, as he told his mother, "the words seem to melt on the page." He also showed symptoms of perceptual immaturity, but these were mild compared to his visual disorders.

We started Brendan on a course of vision therapy that lasted for thirty sessions in our office, plus a set of supplementary home exercises. The purpose of the therapy is to create situations in which the brain is induced to give the right messages to the eyes. To repeat an earlier comparison, this is much like

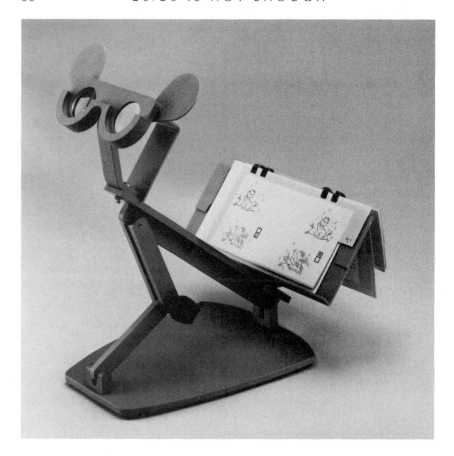

TESTING BINOCULAR SKILLS I

The cheiroscope, shown in the photo, is used both to test and to improve the ability to integrate information from the two eyes. The instrument presents separate images to each eye. The patient is asked to trace with each hand the image that is seen. The tracings reproduced here show the progress in therapy of an adult patient suffering from intermittent divergent strabismus; her left eye turned out. In the center in each case is the image she was asked to reproduce; on each side are what she respectively traced with her left and right hands. In the first tracing, the patient saw nothing at all on the left side and on the right she was able to reproduce only part of the object. In the second she was able to reproduce on the left side, and by the end of therapy, five months later, her binocular skills had improved to the point where she was able accurately to reproduce a clown holding a pig, an image far more complex than those she had previously been tested on.

Photo courtesy of Bernell Corporation, South Bend, Indiana

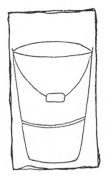 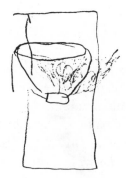

learning a skill such as touch-typing. And, like touch-typing, it takes a lot of practice before it becomes second nature. The visual situations are created with the use of lenses and prisms and various kinds of instruments, some simple, some elaborate. Some of the routines are games that will challenge a patient, whether child or adult.

By about halfway through the course we could observe the improvement in Brendan's visual skills. By the time he began third grade he was finished with his therapy. His visual skills were normal.

The scholastic results of Brendan M.'s therapy can be easily summarized. He started with us late in second grade. By the middle of third grade he was reading at grade level. That same year Brendan won the class reading prize. His attitude was transformed. His parents reported that he was once again the cheerful, self-confident boy he had been before his visual troubles got in his way. As this is written, Brendan is attending an Ivy League college. It it worth noting, finally, that Brendan received no other form of intervention during the time he was having his vision therapy—no psychologist or reading specialist was treating him.

•

In the later years of grade school the demands on children's vision increase dramatically, and the primary problems we encounter are disorders of the visual skills. In the first two grades the child is learning the code that is reading, and his problems if any are usually in his visual perception. He is not called on to do much reading for information. Beginning in third grade, and increasing steadily thereafter, he is expected to read to learn: the skill must be second nature; for the first time in his life he must be able to read for sustained periods. The type in his books is much smaller than the letters on the blocks in first grade, and he has to keep his mind on it for much longer.

In its demands on vision, reading a chapter is radically different from reading a line. The child now confronts the intense close work that A. M. Skeffington, the father of modern vision therapy, called "an affront and insult to the natural and primitive use of eyesight."

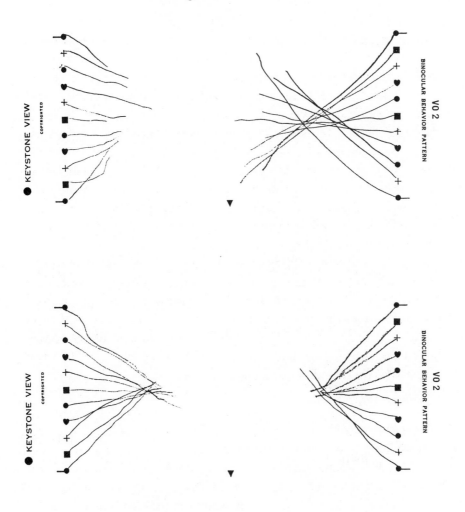

TESTING BINOCULAR SKILLS II

The tracings reproduced here were made with the cheiroscope, the instrument shown on page 60, which displays separate images to each eye. The patient is asked to draw lines simultaneously with her left and right hands so that they appear to meet. The first line starts at the top left for the left hand and at the bottom right for the right hand, the next line one down at left and one up at right, and so on. The patient, who suffered from intermittent strabismus (her left eye turned in), was unable in the first drawing to complete the lines on the left side. She tried to compensate by extending the right lines. Six months later she was able to bring the lines together, demonstrating a great improvement in her binocular vision.

Now even minor flaws in vision—flaws our hunter ancestors, their eyes on the horizon, would never even notice—can prove an insurmountable handicap. These flaws, which typically involve the ability to make the eyes work together, begin to show up when the child has to read the fine print. What are called "saccadic movements" are a good example. When we read, our eyes do not glide smoothly across the page; they move in a series of very short, very rapid, very precise jumps, several times a second and several times a line. Several times a second, the eyes must focus, read, jump, refocus, and read. Flaws in these skills manifest themselves not in the inability to read but in growing discomfort with reading for any amount of time: the child can read a line but not a chapter. Because his eyes do not track words properly, this child when called on to read aloud will embarrass himself by repeating or omitting or stumbling over even familiar words. He is likely to have trouble copying from the board and in sustaining his attention. The symptoms the child reports often show the wearing effects of attempting to read with imperfect vision. About 40 percent of the school-age patients we see report that by late in the school day they are seeing double and many say, like Brendan, that the print seems to swim in and out of focus.

•

ROBBIE C. did fairly well in the first three grades. He was considered a bit slow; he read below grade level, but not far below. His teachers said he was a "very nice boy." The roof fell in when Robbie reached fifth grade. His teacher summoned his mother and told her Robbie was "learning disabled" and a severe discipline problem. She wanted the once-nice boy out of her classroom. He was now two years behind in reading and arithmetic. The school threatened to hold him back.

Robbie's parents took him to a psychologist, who found during testing that the boy was dropping whole phrases when he read aloud. This discovery eventually brought Robbie to us for vision therapy. We found that he suffered from intermittent strabismus: one eye drifted out, came back, drifted out again. This condition is particularly hard for the visual system, because the brain cannot make a lasting adjustment as it can if the eye is consistently turned. He was one or two years behind in his perceptual skills. He said he suffered from eyestrain and that his sight often blurred.

After Robbie had been in vision therapy for nine months, clinical tests showed that his vision was normal. His drifting eye was straight. His skills were now at his age level. In school his arithmetic began to improve right away; the reading came more slowly. In the next three years Robbie picked up the equivalent of five years in his schoolwork. He had caught up. Robbie's life changed in other ways. Before his therapy he had been a clumsy boy who avoided sports and whose leg turned in when he ran. By the end of the third year after his therapy he had become much more physical and was an above-average soccer player.

•

Visual disorders tend to run in families. No one knows if this means the disorders have genetic causes or whether they result from family environment or, perhaps, some of each. Still, the fact remains that if one member of the family has troubled vision, there is a good chance others will also. So we were not entirely surprised when the parents of Robbie C. brought his younger brother to us.

•

KEITH C.'s parents noticed from his birth that one eye was somewhat turned in. But it was only very slightly turned and, since it did not seem to bother him, they did nothing about it. Keith did very well in school. He was well ahead of grade level in all his skills, and he always got good marks. But, his mother recalled, he was a very aggressive, high-strung boy who couldn't sit still and who "seemed to be churning inside."

She brought Keith to us to check his vision. Like his older brother, Keith suffered from intermittent strabismus, but in his case the eye turned in rather than out. Maintaining binocular vision was a constant struggle for him. We suggested vision therapy and we prescribed dual-focus lenses for his glasses.

After a year of therapy, Keith's turned eye is now straight. His visual and perceptual skills test at normal levels. He is much calmer now. "The tension has gone out of his life," his mother said. His formerly severe headaches go away if he remembers to wear his glasses, or, more recently, his contact lenses.

•

Many parents of children who, like Keith, suffer from strabismus have followed an eye doctor's recommendation to have a surgeon operate on the turned eye. Yet it has long been known that this surgery usually produces only a cosmetic result while often leaving the child's vision impaired. The best witness we know on this point is himself an ophthalmologist who performed many such operations. A. D. Reudeman wrote: "Over a period of years, keeping very accurate studies of the end results of ocular muscle surgery, I have been embarrassed and chagrined many times by the tendency of the foveas to revert to their previous positions [that is, the eye went back to its turned position]. The central vision in the operated eye is not maintained and, although the youngster is somewhat improved, many are unable to carry on in school at an intelligence level equal to their age and normal social group." Reudeman said that in his own practice he had "cosmetically straightened 80 percent of my cases" but went on to say that "this is truly a cosmetic result and has little to do with the physio-psychological intellectual level of the individual upon whom this operation has been performed." He said that less than 10 percent of his cases had adequate visual skills after the surgery. In the absence of those skills, he said, surgeons were "developing our own group of neurotics, our own group of people who had nervous breakdowns, and people with inferior intellectual abilities." Reudeman wrote those words in 1953, but today that operation is still being performed. (All this said, we should add in fairness that for at least some patients it is a combination of surgery and therapy—given recent advances in both fields—that produces the best results.)

Sometimes vision therapy succeeds in solving the immediate problem but has to be reinforced later on. This is particularly likely when the visual system is still developing and when the demands on vision are changing radically as they do in the later grades of elementary school. Such was the case with Lindsay G., whom we met in the last chapter when she was four and wearing a patch to treat her lazy left eye.

•

LINDSAY did well in school from the beginning. Her grades were well above average and she was well above grade level in reading and arithmetic. She was a promising young athlete. All went well for the first three grades.

In fourth grade Lindsay began to have serious problems. Her schoolwork continued to be good, but the added amount of reading she had to do was a strain on her. Her mother had to help with homework by reading alternate pages aloud. Lindsay had no trouble reading as such, it was just the amount of it that was hard on her. She pushed aside her glasses, saying they were of no use to her, and rubbed her eyes. She complained of headaches as she had years earlier. She put her face down very close to her work, and when watching television would sit within a foot or two of the set. Her eye practitioner said her lazy left eye was once more not working for her, and he recommended vision therapy. We found that the great difference between the sight in one eye and in the other was causing trouble now that a lot of reading was demanded of her.

Three months of therapy made a change in Lindsay that was quick and dramatic. We succeeded in equalizing the sight in her two eyes. As a result, her headaches were greatly diminished and she was no longer rubbing her eyes. Her grades, always good, now shot up into the upper 90s, and she was on the honor roll although, her mother said, she needed less time for study. She was enjoying reading again and was taking books out of the library. She no longer asked her mother for help in getting through her reading.

Lindsay was once again the happy child she had been before fourth grade, her mother reported. She was even playing vision therapist on weekends, with her friends as her patients. She was looking forward to the next summer's tennis season.

•

Some words of caution are in order lest we seem in these pages to be offering vision therapy as a simple panacea for the very complex problems of children who have trouble with reading. We are well aware that these problems are complex, that the inability to read has many roots, and that our profession does not have all the answers.

Not all reading problems can be attributed to visual disorders. Nor does vision therapy always succeed. Here we should note that success in our field is not an either-or proposition like treating a contagion: either you still have the bug or you don't. Like practicing a skill, vision therapy need not have all-or-nothing results: you can improve your vision a little, quite a bit, or a great deal. So we find that while a few children will drop out or make little noticeable improvement, the great majority end up with visual skills that are at or above normal.

Good vision does not guarantee good reading. Some children whose vision therapy is successful may still need other forms of help —from a psychologist or a reading specialist, for example—in order to catch up in reading. This is especially likely if the child has had a relatively long record of failure before his therapy. When a child is profoundly discouraged about school and learning, the road back is not easy, and clearing away a visual obstacle is not all that must be done to rescue him.

"Vision therapy doesn't teach reading" is a criticism we sometimes hear. Of course it doesn't; if it did, we would put a lot of teachers out of work. Two analogies may clarify what vision therapy can and cannot do. Imagine a nearsighted child who cannot see what the teacher is writing on the blackboard. Fit the child with glasses. That doesn't mean he can read what's up there, but now he can at least see to read it. Or—an analogy that fits Brendan's case—imagine that you must get through a great deal of printed matter for tomorrow's meeting and you have a splitting headache. You take some aspirin. The headache goes away. You still haven't read all that fine print—but now you feel able to tackle it. Like the glasses, like the aspirin, vision therapy can be the first step that makes the rest possible.

And that's a lot.

5

EDUCATION, CAREER CHOICE, AND DELINQUENCY

Education after grade school is a ladder whose rungs are sometimes spaced far apart. At each major change, from grade school to high school, from high school to college, from college to graduate or professional school, the demands on our visual system increase, not gradually but suddenly and dramatically. Sometime during that climb young people choose the career that will occupy their working years —a choice in which the match between work and vision is rarely considered. Along the way a large number of young people will drop off the educational ladder. For too many of them, particularly those who drop out early, their choice will lead them into delinquent behavior and eventually perhaps into a career in crime. The evidence is that the majority of delinquent youths suffer from severe learning-related visual problems, which caused them the trouble in school that led them to drop out—and that treating those visual problems dramatically reduces their chances of committing further offenses against society.

More school means more reading and more stress for the reader's vision. As we've seen, many children run into difficulty about the time they are in fourth grade because their vision, good enough for learning to read, is not good enough for reading to learn. The problem becomes greater in later years. High school brings a quantum jump in required reading. The amount will vary according to schools and course of study, but usually a high school student is expected to read several times as much every day as he did in the earlier grades. Now some students who did well in the earlier years find themselves in

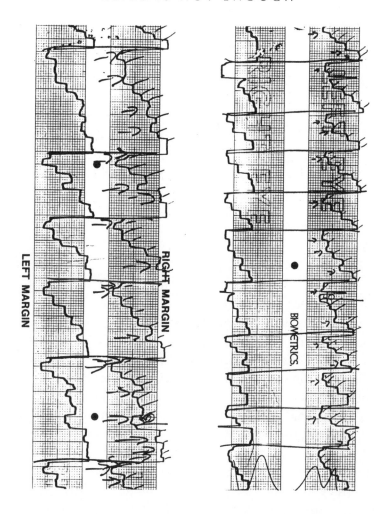

HOW THE EYES MOVE WHILE READING

An instrument called a reading eye camera records the movements of a patient's eyes while reading. Each vertical segment shows the movement of each eye across a single line of type. The arrows on the graph at right show how many times the patient had to stop and look back—four times in the first line. The record of eye movements is combined with reading comprehension to give a measure known as "reading efficiency." At seventeen, this high school senior's reading efficiency was on an eighth-grade level. For every 100 words he read, he moved his eyes 77 times and had to go back 37 times. He read 192 words a minute with a comprehension of 60 percent. The second graph shows his results after seven months of therapy. Now for every 100 words read, he moved his eyes only 58 times and went back only 17 times. He read 393 words a minute with 90 percent comprehension. His reading efficiency was now at college level.

deep water. Their vision cannot handle the sudden flood of printed matter. Some who had been good students become failures, to their own and others' distress. Vision is not easily identified as the culprit. This student after all read perfectly well before, but now he says he can't concentrate or is always tired or that he hates school. His failure is all the more exasperating to parents and teachers for having no apparent cause. You can't help wondering: is he really trying? The parents are frustrated, the teacher is frustrated, the student especially is frustrated, and these frustrations create fertile soil for emotional problems.

One such parent was himself a man of enormous energy and determination: Lyndon B. Johnson, then vice-president and soon to be president. At sixteen, his daughter Luci was in serious trouble at school. She was an intelligent girl and did her work diligently. But hard work got her nowhere; her grades were poor. Written work she was proud of turned out to be full of errors she had not seen. Her coordination was poor, and in games she was usually the last to be chosen. Luci Johnson was on the verge of dropping out of school.

No one could figure out what was wrong with Luci. Not her sight, surely, for she tested regularly at 20/20 on the Snellen chart. Nonetheless, after Luci had blacked out in school during a test, the White House physician suggested she see Dr. Robert A. Kraskin, a Washington optometrist who included vision therapy in his practice. Kraskin found that Luci's eye coordination was very poor. This accounted for the difficulty she had reading or doing written work and her frustrating inability to see the errors in her own writing. She began vision therapy.

Years later Luci recalled that at first she had been a recalcitrant patient. But she persisted, and her therapy began to pay off in better schoolwork. In eighteen months her grades went from D's to B's. She went on to college and in her freshman year she made the honor roll. "For someone who had been on scholastic probation so long, this achievement was a thrilling one indeed," she observed later. She also noticed that her physical coordination was better.

Luci Johnson retained an interest in the subject after her own therapy was successfully completed. She worked for two years as an assistant in Dr. Kraskin's office. Currently she is president of Volunteers for Vision, Inc., a national organization whose primary goal is to establish a preschool vision-screening program. She summed up the lessons of her experience in these words: "If the key to a better society is a better education, then the key to a better education is better vision. If you don't have that key, you can't open the door to a better life."

•

When SHARI M. came to us she was a bright, lively girl of fifteen, but she was failing her first year in high school. She knew how to read but she read too slowly to keep up with her work, and her attention was poor. "I could read a book for fifteen minutes, then I'd lose all concentration," she said. And if she read for an hour her eyes began to hurt. Her sight tested at 20/20, but when we examined her we found she had difficulty aligning her eyes together on a target and holding them there. That was why reading for any length of time was hard for her. Shari began a program of vision therapy that was to last six months.

The summer between her freshman and sophomore years Shari began to notice she was making progress. She went to summer school. She recalled: "The teacher would give us work. Other kids did it in an hour, but I did it in half an hour." By that fall we found that her visual skills were normal. With the impediment to her vision removed, Shari's schoolwork improved enormously. Where the previous year she had been failing, now she was getting A's and B's. She could read much longer at a stretch without losing her concentration. Shari noticed that her classmates viewed her differently. "Before they thought, well, she's just Shari, but now they think I'm smart," she observed. "Now I love school."

•

JULIE R. was also fifteen and in her first year of high school. She had always had problems with school, but now with the added demands of high school her problems were becoming acute. She was in a remedial class and, her mother said, she was "falling further and further behind." She could not concentrate on her homework. She would lose her place when reading, skip

•

words, and have to reread sentences; she confused letters and similar-seeming words. She found it hard to remember what she'd read. Reading fatigued Julie, and any kind of close work made her feel tense. When she was reading, her mother noticed, Julie would turn her head and read with only one eye.

We found that Julie was suffering from divergent strabismus —one eye that turned out. The turn was not normally visible, though her mother had noticed it in school pictures. Her eye movements were jumpy and uneven. Sometimes she saw double. Her visual skills were four years behind the norm for her age. On a test for figure-ground perception known as the Southern California Test, her ability to pick out visual patterns was that of a nine-year-old. This test measures the ability to separate some information (the figure) from other, surrounding information (the ground). A student with poor figure-ground perception will have trouble, for example, with a page that includes many arithmetic problems because she cannot concentrate on one single problem to the exclusion of the rest.

Julie started therapy at the beginning of her sophomore year. By spring the improvement in her vision was noticeable. Her double vision was gone. The formerly turned eye was now straight, and she had caught up in her visual skills. Her figure-ground score was normal. Julie was doing much better in school. She was still somewhat behind her peers but was no longer losing ground. She no longer complained about school, and was confident that she could compete on even terms. For the first time, Julie was reading for pleasure. Before, she used to start a book but quickly put it aside. Now she would take a book from the library and finish it.

•

At college, the next rung on the ladder of education, the demand on students' vision makes another quantum leap. Again depending on the college and course of study, young people will now have to read from twice to five times as much as they did in high school. Most students who choose to go on to college recognize that academic success is their main job at this stage in their lives. To achieve that success, they need a visual system that enables them: (1) to read

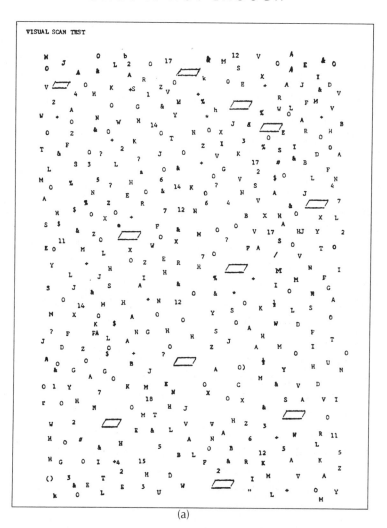

(a)

VISUAL SCANNING

In this test (a) the patient is asked to connect as many of the "o"s as he can in 60 seconds. The test shows how effectively the person uses his eyes to scan the symbols on a page. The patient in this case, a fifteen-year-old, was reading at a ten-year-old level. In the first test (b) he was able to connect 34 "o"s. Note also the pattern of the connecting lines, which reveals that he was scanning the page up and down. In the second test (c), after therapy, he was able to connect 57 "o"s, almost 70 percent more than the first time. This time, moreover, the pattern shows that he scanned the page from left to right, as one does while reading. The visual scanning test was devised by Dr. Morton Davis.

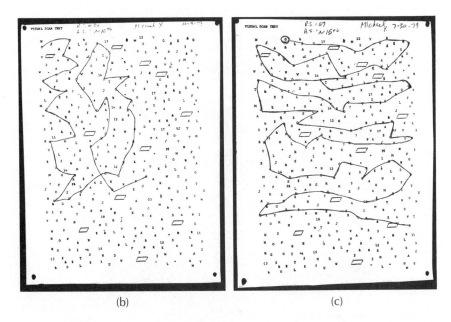

(b)   (c)

comfortably and rapidly for long stretches of time, (2) to keep their attention concentrated for all that time, (3) to process the information contained in what they are reading quickly and accurately, and (4) to store it accurately and efficiently for quick retrieval. That is asking a lot of our vision.

Since at least 80 percent of learning comes through the eyes, a better visual system will greatly enhance a student's chances of success in college and in later life. On the other hand, the tolerance for visual failure is much less than it was in high school. The student who got through high school without doing the reading by listening attentively in class finds that this strategy no longer works in college: the professor doesn't cover the reading in class. A minor flaw in vision is enough to damage or even ruin a student's college career. Again, it is not easy to see that the problem is visual, for his complaint will typically be not about the eyes but instead about being unable to concentrate on his work or feeling generally uncomfortable while studying. As we've noted, most eye doctors in any event do not even test for this kind of visual problem. The effect of such a visual flaw need not be as dramatic as abandoning higher education. For each college student who drops out there are many others who fight their way through despite the handicap and go on to a career that demands

TREATING STRABISMUS

As a child (photo above), Claudette O. suffered from a visibly turned left eye. She was fifteen when she came to us for vision therapy. She said she saw double "all the time" and was afflicted with headaches. She was doing badly in school and reading was difficult for her. She had little hope of realizing her ambition to become a lawyer. Her first copyform (above) was dramatic confirmation that she was seeing double. She entered a twice-weekly course of therapy that lasted for six months. The photo on p. 77 shows Claudette after her therapy. Her later copyform shows that the double vision has disappeared. She herself reported: "I don't see double anymore, no headaches, concentration improved, my grades are much better. I read a lot more and play piano better. It's easier to play cards and watch television. Overall," she concluded, "everything has improved."

visually intensive close work. Yet, though they may manage in school and career, they will pay a high price for an untreated defect in vision. In a competitive world, they will be pitted against rivals who are more comfortable with intensive close work and do it more efficiently and are therefore more likely to make that added winning effort. To the extent that they do succeed in their work, they will pay a much steeper price for their success than do less talented people with better vision. That price comes in the form of chronic discomfort and strain that often makes its victim irritable and hostile—ask the spouse! All this because of a visual problem that could have been solved if only the question had been asked.

· · ·

The choice of a career is one of life's most important decisions. At no other time can we observe so clearly the mismatch between the eyes that nature gave us and the vision that the world requires of us. Most of us are born with our hunting ancestors' eyes, designed for scanning the distant horizon, but the modern economy wants us to have desk worker's eyes that are suited to focusing all day within arm's length. We cannot go back to the prehistoric world for which our eyes were designed, so we must adapt to the present as best we can. We could —indeed we must—adapt a lot better than we do if we are to live in the world of the present.

Different occupations call on different visual skills, and different occupations subject people to different kinds of visual stress. Only at the extremes are the visual requirements of a given type of work obvious. Everyone knows that a pilot must have excellent distant vision, and equally good depth perception to make the key spatial judgments involved in landing. Few, however, may realize that he also needs equally good focusing skill to switch his attention rapidly to and from the skies ahead, the dials in front of him, and his sets of written instructions.

Despite the modern trend toward sustained close-up work, there are still plenty of occupations well suited to hunter's eyes. Most people-related jobs are in this category. In work connected with people, the visual zone of most importance—the place where keen perception is critical—is well beyond reading distance. Sales is a good example. A salesman reads people not books, and he must do it accurately and sensitively at some distance. Like his ancestors, the salesman makes his kill beyond arm's length. Many business executives also do their most important work with people rather than papers, across a conference table rather than at a desk. Police, firefighting, social work are all distant-vision kinds of work. Politics is an extreme case. A candidate appealing to a crowd has his perceptions focused at a great distance: he will win or lose on the quality of that distant perception rather than on anything he does close up. No one ever got to the White House just on his reading skill. Many presidents no doubt have been good readers, but they have owed their success to other kinds of visual skills.

The variety of visual skills is much greater than just an adaptation for close or distant work. In Chapter 9 we describe the subtle differences among the visual skills needed by professionals in different sports. Every sport is somewhat different in its visual demands, and usually there are differences even within a sport between one position and another. In this intensely competitive world, where if you are not extremely good you are out of a job, the would-be professional can be fatally handicapped for lack of just the right kind of visual skill. Similarly, in law a litigator with excellent speaking skills may depend on a colleague with better reading skills to prepare the case he will present.

Similar subtle differences exist among various kinds of close visual work. People who work all day with words or numbers—lawyers, accountants, stenographers, academics, editors—perform in an essentially two-dimensional world. Depth perception, peripheral vision, and dynamic vision (vision in motion) are not critical to their ability to earn a living. Not so for the surgeon and particularly the dentist: their work is highly three-dimensional and demands excellent eye-hand coordination. The dentist spends his working life in a small room doing highly precise handwork about fifteen inches from his eyes; the distances are very small, and the tolerance for error is virtually zero. The surgeon needs the same visual and eye-hand skills, but the dentist needs an added tolerance for confined visual work, for he spends all day in that small room whereas the surgeon spends much of his time away from the operating table. Still, a visual problem need not bar someone from a chosen career, even as a surgeon or dentist, if the problem is successfully treated:

●

CARL B. barely got through high school. He had great trouble doing his homework. When he read, his eyes would soon begin to hurt, he got headaches, and he fell asleep over the book. It was hard to concentrate. He had wanted since ninth grade to become a dentist. Now, with eight more years of education ahead, he knew he would have trouble with all the reading that was in store if he was to follow his chosen career.

We found that Carl had difficulty aligning his eyes on a close target and keeping them there for any length of time—just the

visual skill needed by a dentist. In the summer before he entered
college, Carl followed an intensive course of vision therapy. His
eyes now aligned normally. By the time he was in college his
headaches were gone and he was able to read for three hours at
a stretch without losing his concentration. He did well in college
and went on to master the visual demands of four years in dental
school. He still considers himself a somewhat slow reader, but
he was able to handle all the work his education required of him.
When we last saw him, Carl B. had just finished dental school
and was about to go into practice.

●

Radiology is also close work, but what it requires is excellent visual
perception. When radiologists read X rays they search for the abnormal pattern that indicates a problem and its severity. People with
otherwise good sight vary greatly in their aptitude for visual perception. Once you think about it, this is a commonplace reality. We all
know that some of us recognize faces and patterns, or find lost objects,
far better than others. But this commonplace is seldom if ever considered in choosing a career in radiology.

Young people on the verge of choosing a career would do well to
give more than passing thought to the match between their own vision
and the demands of a given occupation. If they can find visual guidance in making that choice, they should call on it. Good vision is an
asset in any walk of life, but, as we've seen, in any kind of work some
visual skills are going to be more important than others. The questions to ask are: Where is my vision going to be concentrated? Think
of the world as a series of visual zones and ask, Where out there, in
which of those zones, is it most important that my visual understanding of the world be at its best? What particular visual and visually
related skills will I most need? And am I going to be comfortable
doing that all day long? Obviously there are many other considerations involved in choosing a career, and people will not always be able
to make a perfect match between vision and work, if only because the
world no longer needs so many hunters. But if they ask the right
questions, young people should be able at the very least to avoid a
painful mismatch. It is not enough to dismiss the issue with some
thought like: "I can take it for eight hours a day, and for the rest of

my time it doesn't really matter." For one thing, a person who is visually ill suited for his work is likely to do poorly at it as compared to competitors who suffer no such handicap. For another, doing the wrong kind of visual work often causes chronic stress that cannot be left at the office but will carry over to diminish the quality of the rest of a person's life. This is brought home to us in our practice. Often we will hear a patient talk about the strain of close desk work—and then we hear the spouse talk with intense feeling about how hard it is to live with that person after his day at the office.

Educational institutions do next to nothing to help young people find the right visual direction. It is a rare guidance counselor who includes visual aptitude as a factor in his advice to students. Professional schools do no better in selecting their students. Dentistry is again a good example. One might think that schools training for this of all jobs would pay careful attention to their applicants' visual skills, but such is not the case. People are admitted to dental school mainly on grades won by reading and writing skills for which they will have little need in practice. The skills they will need at work—excellent eye-hand coordination and spatial perception—bear little relation to the visual skills they have demonstrated in school. Some dental schools do give a superficial test of manual dexterity, such as carving a piece of chalk, but that's all.

•

BEN C. is a senior accountant. In his forties he became aware that he was under increasing stress. He would come home "wound tight as a spring," and it would take him an hour to relax. He avoided reading at home. He realized that he was also avoiding desk work on the job. He would walk over to another office to get information he could have gotten over the phone— just to get away from his desk. He would ask for information orally that he could have gotten in writing. His habits were noticed. Colleagues would comment that he spent a lot of time out of his office.

Ben C. came to us for vision therapy. His troubles with close work were caused, we found, by the difficulty his visual system had in bringing his eyes together on a single target and holding them there—a condition known as convergence insufficiency.

The therapy cured his convergence problem, and his symptoms went away. Once he was aware of the causes of his visual stress, Ben C. took the drastic step of changing careers. He gave up accounting and took a position in which he only has about four hours a day of work with figures. Moreover, he can schedule that work himself. He also is more comfortable away from work. He is reading for pleasure.

As he looks back over his life, Ben C. wishes he had chosen a career that demanded less intensive close work than accountancy. Something to do with finance or investment. He realizes now that there were warning signals when he was in college: he had trouble with courses like English and history that require a lot of reading. But at the time he did not know what those signals were saying about his future, and there was no one else around to tell him.

•

Crime is a form of career choice. In most cases it starts with dropping out of school, followed by juvenile delinquency of one kind or another. The progression from the problem child who disrupts a classroom to the young thug who disrupts a neighborhood is a sadly familiar story of our times. The dropout finds that the modern world offers few good jobs this side of the law. Crime becomes a tempting career choice for someone who may see a lifetime behind a fast-food counter as the likely alternative.

The link between trouble in school and trouble on the street is thoroughly documented. Any number of studies have offered statistical proof of what instinct suggests: the great majority of juvenile delinquents (estimates range up to 80 percent) suffer from more or less severe learning disabilities. That knowledge, along with concern about violent crime, has led to a variety of institutional teaching programs designed to get incarcerated youths back into school on their release. But all too often these efforts come up against the same barrier that blocks many remedial school programs: the young people they seek to teach are fatally handicapped by visual problems. The teacher's task—and the student's—is harder when the student is older. The students are after all being asked to try again at what they failed before, and if failure is painful at age ten it is all the more so when repeated at eighteen.

THE COMPUTER IN VISION TESTING

The computer is a versatile tool in vision therapy. Here it is being used to test the patient's binocular skills. The patient is wearing glasses with one red and one green lens, which causes him to see images on the screen separately with each eye. To see the complete image the brain must receive messages from both eyes. If one eye is suppressing information, as is common when binocular skills are faulty, the patient will fail to see a complete image. The patient registers what he sees by pressing the button in his left hand. The box on top of the computer provides the therapist with an objective reading (in a printout) of the patient's performance.

In the case of young delinquents, their visual handicaps are unusually severe. This too has been documented by research going back more than twenty years. In the mid-1960s Dr. David Dzik of Chattanooga surveyed the vision of youths who came before the juvenile court of Hamilton County, Tennessee. Dzik found that almost three-quarters, 72 percent, failed one or more of the vision tests he gave them. Ten years later members of five professions, including optometry, studied a group of juvenile delinquents in Richmond, Virginia. The optometrist, Michael Etkin, reported: "Virtually every subject had vision problems of some kind. [There was] a complete permeation of vision problems throughout the structure of the study." Also in the 1970s, Dr. Roger Dowis of Boulder, Colorado, took the research one step further. He ran a pilot vision-treatment program for juvenile offenders that succeeded in reducing their recidivism rate (measured by whether they completed two years of parole without further incident) to 4 percent compared to 18 percent among those who received no vision care. Two other researchers—Joel N. Zaba, an optometrist, and Gary H. Bachara, a psychologist—combined vision therapy with other kinds of help for a group of juvenile offenders in the Tidewater area of Virginia. They found that when the young delinquents were offered both vision therapy as needed and other help for their learning disabilities, the rate of recidivism dropped to 6 percent, compared to 42 percent for a control group that received neither kind of help.

Thus the connection between visual problems and delinquent behavior has been well documented for a good number of years. Yet this accumulated evidence has been seldom recognized and still less often acted upon.

A notable exception is the highly successful program started by Dr. Stanley Kaseno. Kaseno is an optometrist in San Bernardino, California, with a practice in vision therapy, an interest in young people, and an awareness of the work of David Dzik and others. In the late 1970s Kaseno decided to try to put it all together in the form of a clinic to treat the visual needs of young people incarcerated at the San Bernardino Juvenile Hall, the local place of detention. He then spent three discouraging years knocking on the doors of funding sources before he was at last able to find financing for what he wanted to do.

The vision clinic at San Bernardino Juvenile Hall began seeing patients on July 14, 1980, and at this writing is operating as a permanent fixture. The young people Kaseno found there averaged just over sixteen years of age, and nine out of ten of them were male. They were far behind in their school skills. Tests showed them functioning six years below grade level.

When Kaseno's staff examined them, they found that almost all of the young people in the juvenile hall had visual problems that had not been diagnosed or treated. They were unable to make effective use of their eyes. Most were deficient in the basic skills of eye movement and focusing, and the great majority showed such symptoms as headaches, short attention span, and poor comprehension. Those who could read at all could do so for only five or ten minutes.

In the clinic's first five years its staff prescribed glasses for almost half its patients. But of these only 20 percent were for the usual refractive errors of near- and farsightedness and astigmatism. The rest were therapeutic lenses designed to reduce the stress of close work for youths who had no trouble seeing at distance—their hunter's eyes were all too well adapted to a life of street crime.

About an equal number of young offenders were put into a course of vision therapy that typically lasts for twenty-four half-hour sessions over twelve weeks. This course is the heart of the clinic's mission as Stanley Kaseno conceived it.

Vision therapy at San Bernardino has been a great success by any measure. By the measure that most concerns society—will they stop committing crimes?—the program has greatly increased the chance that its graduates will go straight. The rate of recidivism among the inmates overall (measured by whether they were charged with another offense during their first six months out) had been running from 50 to 60 percent. Among those who complete vision therapy the rate of repeat offenses has run between 10 and 15 percent. Given that it costs about $29,000 to keep a young offender at San Bernardino for a year, the vision clinic represents a big saving in money alone. The greater saving is the reduction in the fear and suffering and wasted lives that are the price society pays for violent crime.

According to the standards of school, the vision therapy program has been equally successful. The school skills of those who completed therapy showed a remarkable increase. When they were tested after therapy, youths who had been functioning at a fifth-grade level scored on the average at a grade level of 8.5—a gain of more than three years in a few months. This was accomplished without any added academic instruction. A veteran reading teacher at San Bernardino said: "I've seen kids' grade levels immediately rise two and three levels."

The young people at San Bernardino have taken readily to vision therapy. After an initial period of suspicion they began to come voluntarily, and some referred their friends. No doubt Stanley Kaseno's dedication and personality have a lot to do with the clinic's early acceptance. Kaseno has been careful to design courses of therapy that always build on success rather than confronting an inmate with still another failure. Some of the devices, such as a kind of trampoline used to practice vision in motion, are appealing to active young males. The activities in vision therapy have the advantage of not resembling the classroom routines at which they have so regularly failed. Finally, vision therapy has the further advantage that, unlike psychological counseling, it does not invade the patient's privacy.

The stories of two youths, recounted by Blanch Brandt, administrator of the vision program, illustrate the complexities involved in dealing with gang members. Chico, seventeen, had been incarcerated for the third time. He had finished eleventh grade, then dropped out of school. He said to Mrs. Brandt: "Blanch, I have spent many hours during the past week thinking back from the time I first went to school to the time things started to go wrong in my life. The one thing which really hit home was that I just don't have the confidence or guts to say no, and I end up going along with my friends. I feel like I am just a follower and that I get used by my so-called friends a lot of the time." When he was examined, Chico said reading made his eyes hurt, the words would start to blur, he would get headaches and sometimes double vision. He entered a course of vision therapy aimed at improving his poor focusing and eye-teaming skills. His progress was excellent. After the therapy, he said he had no trouble reading, and his achievement test showed an increase of six grade levels. About a year after leaving San Bernardino, Chico returned to show Mrs. Brandt a certificate attesting to his successful completion of a 270-hour course to be an emergency medical technician. He was starting work the following Monday. His outlook on life had changed; he was no longer a follower. He told Mrs. Brandt: "Now I choose my friends, and I have the guts to say right up front that friendship does not have to be conditional."

Chico escaped the gang environment. Willy did not. At sixteen, Willy was a chronic offender who had already been in the Juvenile Hall ten times. He had finished tenth grade but tested at the sixth-grade level. At his examination, Willy also said words blurred when he read, he would lose his place and find himself reading the same line over and over, and his eyes would begin to hurt. He entered vision therapy designed to improve his focusing and his jerky and inaccurate eye movements. Willy's progress was truly spectacular. Six months later he tested no less than ten reading levels higher than before his therapy. After leaving San Bernardino, Willy asked his probation officer for permission to move north where he could find a job and not be around his former friends or gang. A few months later Mrs. Brandt learned that Willy had been murdered and that his killing was believed to be "gang-related." It had happened when he came home, for the first time, for a family celebration.

San Bernardino's record makes it an established success, a proven way to combat juvenile crime. Its demonstrated accomplishment has inspired some others. In New Orleans, for example, a vision clinic was opened in 1983 at the Jackson Heights Barracks, where juveniles are held. There are others, but they are still far too few.

More—much more—remains to be done. We now know enough to say with certainty that vision therapy is an effective way to turn many young offenders away from a career in crime. We believe it should be a part of every program for juvenile delinquents.

6

THE WORKPLACE AND
THE VIDEO DISPLAY TERMINAL

Tarzan sits all day in a tiny cubicle staring into a video display terminal. That picture sums up the plight of the many millions of people
who work in an environment that is hostile to the vision with which
nature endowed them.

As we know, in the modern world most people earn their living
doing some kind of desk work. Among them are many whose eyes,
adapted to distant vision, will suffer to a greater or lesser degree from
being focused all day at arm's length. For a rapidly increasing number
of people, close work involves using a video display terminal for part
or all of the day. For all its undoubted economic value, the VDT has
made a bad visual situation considerably worse.

•

DAVID H. is an editor. Nearsighted, he has worn glasses since
his early teens, and now, in his sixties, the glasses are bifocals.
He has been an avid reader since childhood. Doing his work
successfully depends first of all on his ability to read rapidly and
comfortably for hours on end. Much of his time is spent at a
VDT. Until recently, reading presented no problem. He read
all day at his work and then would spend the evening reading
for pleasure.

In his early sixties, David H. noticed that his capacity for
reading was diminishing. In the late afternoon his eyes would
begin to feel uncomfortable. His sight would blur so that it was
both difficult and painful to follow the words on the page. His

right eye was particularly troublesome. It was sore and teary; it
didn't seem to function properly much of the time. When he
was tired, his eyes drifted apart and he was seeing a double
image. He was fidgety and restless. He tried to force himself to
go on working, but some days he would have to give up. Nor
could he read for pleasure as he once did. Now in the evening
he would put down his book after a couple of pages and wander
around looking for something to do. He found his productivity
falling and feared that his income would follow suit.

Our examination showed that David H. had "divergence excess": his eyes turned out easily but found it difficult—increasingly so with age—to turn in. He was seeing with both eyes
only intermittently; much of the time his weaker right eye was
not functioning. This is the beginning of amblyopia, the loss of
sight in one eye because the brain, to rid itself of an unwanted
double image, rejects one of the images. Untreated, this can
result in severe loss of sight in the rejected eye.

After six months of therapy, David H.'s vision was much
improved. Most of his exercises were designed to give him better
control over his eye movements. In other exercises his eyes
worked separately, so that to see the whole picture he had to use
both eyes. This was intended to induce the brain to register the
messages of the weak right eye. He began to report improvement
after three months and after another three said that he was now
content with his vision. He said he was once more able to put in
a full day at his desk without discomfort and read in the evening
besides. He no longer felt his eyes drifting apart, and his sight
seldom blurred. His right eye no longer bothered him. It didn't
get irritated late in the day, and he didn't have the feeling that it
was not seeing as well as his left eye. Our tests confirmed these
reports: he was better able to manage his eye movements, and
the intermittent suppression of sight in the right eye was gone.
The sight in his right eye was improved. His two eyes saw
equally well with the same prescription he'd had when he came
to us.

Much of the improvement in David H.'s vision was due to
the greater control his therapy gave him over the coordination of
his eyes. But he also practiced strategies we suggested for mini-

mizing visual stress. His desk, fortunately, is by a big window with a view that stretches off for a couple of miles. David H. now makes it a practice to stop every so often, lift his eyes, and gaze out the window at the most distant objects he can see. He need not interrupt his train of thought; he can think about what he's doing while he gazes at the horizon. He has learned also that he can dispel occasional blurring by shifting his focus rapidly back and forth between the words on the page and, say, a painting on the wall. These two strategies, gazing away and shifting focus, clear his sight and allow him to go on working without discomfort.

●

Dentists work under conditions of potentially high visual stress. They need excellent eye-hand coordination and, above all, accurate depth perception to gauge the very small distances within which they work. Failing depth perception brought one dentist to us for vision therapy:

●

ERVIN N. was thirty-eight when he first noticed the signs that his depth perception was not as good as it had been. When he sewed up a cut after surgery he was having trouble finding the end of the thread. When giving an injection he would sometimes miss the mark by a few millimeters. Sometimes when he was tired he would see double. In retrospect, but not at the time, Ervin N. realized that he had been avoiding using his left eye. He would seat himself in relation to the patient so as to rely on his right eye. "I was going very monocular," he recalled. That was the root of his problem, since binocular vision—the two eyes working as a team—is what makes depth perception possible.

We found that his eyes were doubly turned. Both eyes drifted out, but his left eye also would turn up. He was getting a double form of double vision: double images, separated both from side to side and up and down. Keeping a single image was a constant struggle. Ervin N. began a course of vision therapy that lasted six months. The therapy eliminated his lateral strabismus: his eyes no longer tended to drift out. But vertical strabismus does not always respond to therapy. His left eye still turned up. We compensated for the upward turn by adding a prism to the prescription in his glasses.

The therapy strengthened Ervin N.'s left eye and thus helped him make his two eyes work as a team. He no longer avoided using his left eye, and his occasional double vision disappeared. Most important, he no longer experienced any visual problem in his work. Ervin N. once more had the excellent depth perception that his profession requires.

•

So far we have discussed visual problems as they apply to the individual. But in some occupations an untreated visual defect can also be a hazard to the general public. In the case of an airline pilot, the point needs no underlining by us. The same applies to the much larger numbers who drive any kind of vehicle on the highway, a subject we take up in Chapter 7. Dentists and surgeons whose vision is troubled are more likely to make mistakes with serious consequences for their patients. In all these examples, the problem is not necessarily with the person's sight. Visual stress leaves a person in less than the best condition to make vital decisions. A dentist or a surgeon who is suffering headaches or eyestrain or general tension because of his visual environment is not going to be at his best when the critical moment comes—even if he checks out perfectly on the eye chart.

Far less familiar is the case of the radiologist. Radiologists are the medical doctors who read our X rays and, on the basis of what they see there, decide if there is a problem that needs medical attention. In many cases that reading of the X ray is the decisive factor in whether the patient gets timely treatment.

Studies of the readings made by radiologists have produced results that are truly alarming. Three steps go into reading an X ray: taking the picture, perceiving what it shows, and interpreting that evidence. The first and third steps—the technology of taking the picture and the interpretation of the evidence—have received considerable attention. The second step, perception, has been little studied, and yet it is there that most mistakes are made.

In 1977 Dr. Frederick Taber, himself a radiologist, summarized the results of a series of studies. One study compared five radiologists' interpretations of the same 1,256 X-ray films. The difference in their positive diagnoses ("positive" meaning a problem that needed attention) ranged from a low of 56 to a high of 100, with the other three in between. Three months later the same five radiologists were asked to read the same X rays again. Now each radiologist disagreed with his own previous reading of the positive cases one time in five on the average. Startled by this outcome, two other researchers staged their own experiments and got similar results. In another study, this time of chest X rays, the researcher found that eight radiologists and chest specialists missed one-quarter of the cases that another expert panel had found were "clinically urgent." In still another study, two radiologists disagreed in 30 percent of the cases, and each one on later reading disagreed with himself 20 percent of the time.

All this is bound to be disturbing, if not downright terrifying, to anyone whose life may hang on a radiologist's reading of his or her X ray. One researcher, speaking to his fellow radiologists, offered in self-defense evidence that other forms of medical diagnosis are at least as prone to error as radiology. That may be of some comfort to radiologists, but obviously it does nothing at all for the rest of us.

Not all job-related vision problems involve close work. The large category of strabismus (turned eye) and amblyopia (lazy eye) can make life difficult for people whose occupation does not center on reading or other kinds of arm's-length work. Those two ailments together afflict 5 to 6 percent of the United States population. As we noted earlier, orthoptics, the ancestor of today's vision therapy, was born in the early nineteenth century when the French ophthalmologist Emile Javal rebelled against the surgery then practiced for strabismus. But the surgical treatment persisted, and still persists today, despite the vast accumulation of evidence showing that it frequently provides dismal results. Surgery can often correct the cosmetic problem, but in the great majority of patients it does not correct the patient's visual problem. The eye that was turned may now appear to be properly aligned, but the patient still does not have adequate binocular vision: the two eyes do not work together as a team. The eyes look right but do not work right. In the large number of people who suffer from strabismus without a visibly turned eye, surgery is unlikely to be of any help at all—there being no cosmetic problem to correct—and indeed is likely only to weaken the muscles of the eye.

Yet all too often surgery is still practiced in such cases. An example
is Gretchen S.:

•

GRETCHEN S. was in her early forties when she began to have
very serious trouble with her vision. She wore glasses for nearsightedness, but her new problems could not be corrected by
glasses. When she tried to look down, her eyes would not work
together and she saw double. She had to tip her head to one side
to get a single image and then her neck began to ache. She could
go downstairs only by closing one eye and holding on to a rail-
ing. She could read only by holding the paper straight out in
front of her. She found herself bumping into things, and she
suffered occasional falls. Driving was difficult and chancy; she
had two accidents in one year.

Worst of all, Gretchen S. found herself unable to function in
her work as a physical therapist. Her peripheral vision had become so poor she could not keep track of what was going on in a
room full of her patients. She could not keep up with the necessary paperwork. Very reluctantly, she gave up a career to which
she had devoted many years and took up less visually demanding
work as a massage therapist.

Gretchen S. made the rounds of eye doctors, seeking help.
An ophthalmologist recommended surgery, and she was operated on in February 1982. The surgery helped somewhat, she
said, but the basic problems remained unchanged. She still
could not look down more than 20 to 30 degrees without seeing
double. "It was not what I'd hoped for," she recalled. Again she
consulted a series of eye specialists. Again they had nothing to
recommend but more surgery. Again she was operated on, this
time in March 1986. This second operation changed nothing at
all, she said: all her problems were as bad as before. Once more
she made the rounds of the doctors. One surgeon recommended
still another operation, with, he said, a "fifty-fifty" chance of
success. But Gretchen S. rebelled at that prospect; she kept on
asking. Eventually a psychologist working in vocational rehabilitation suggested she try vision therapy, and she came to us. We
had to tell her that with the damage done to her eye muscles by

> "You got the biggest piece," said the
> girl. Nobody answered. Nobody looked at
> the little fairy.
> "Both of you got more than I did,"
> said the smallest child. "I want more!"
> The children are looking
> at their plates.
> The three children howled. The
> mother scolded. The father beat "You got the piece of turkey I wanted"
> said the boy.
> on the table with a spoon. What a noise!
> "You got the biggest piece," said the
> "This cannot be Thanksgiving," said the
> girl.
> said the fairy. "This is not fun.
> "Both of you got more than I did,"
> I do not like it.

DOUBLE VISION
Simulation of person seeing double while reading.

two operations her chances were none too promising. Vertical imbalance like hers is at best hard to treat. Such an imbalance combined with the negative effects of surgery made hers potentially one of our most difficult cases. She decided to try anyway, and we started a course of vision therapy.

After six months Gretchen S.'s vision was considerably improved. Her eyes worked together better, and she could look down as much as 40 degrees without seeing double. She could read without holding the paper as high as she did before, and she could tolerate more paperwork. Her peripheral vision, still limited, was considerably improved. Driving was less difficult, though she still had to be extra careful. She felt more confident and was not so unhappy with her vision. "I have much more confidence when I use my eyes," she said. "Life is not nearly as stressful as it was." She estimated that her vision had come about one-half of the way back to what it had been before her troubles began.

Gretchen S. is bitter about what the surgeons did to her. She recalls that she asked them time and again if there were any exercises she could do that might help her vision, a natural question for a physical therapist to ask. Always the answer was no. "Why didn't they tell me about vision therapy?" she asks.

•

A special category among people with job-related visual problems includes those who take up a visually demanding career after years spent in another kind of life. Typically these are women who have spent most of their twenties and perhaps thirties raising a family and keeping a home. Demanding as that life surely is, it does not take a lot of intense close visual work. If such a person returns to work, or often school followed by work, she may find that her vision is not up to the sudden new demand for a lot of arm's-length visual concentration. An example is Julie O.:

•

JULIE O. had raised three children when she decided to go back to work. The career in family therapy that she wanted to pursue meant she would have to take a master's degree, then enter a doctoral program that would require a great deal more reading than she had had to do in college. Once she was a full-time student again, after many years away from the books, she found she was having trouble with the quantity of graduate-level reading. Her attention span was limited. It was hard to focus in the mornings. Because she had to put so much energy into focusing her eyes, she did not have enough left to focus in the intellectual sense. She worried about the years of even heavier reading that lay ahead. Could she keep up with her much younger fellow students?

We found she had a mild form of divergent strabismus: one eye drifted out from time to time. Julie O. then took twenty hours of vision therapy over the summer before she was to enter her doctoral program.

Julie O. found that she could function better as a student after her therapy. Her eyes no longer bothered her when she was studying. The problem of focusing in the mornings vanished. "Because I no longer had to think about my eyes, I had much more energy to think about the subject," she said. She could read for longer periods at a stretch. Like David H., she took to heart our advice on ways to limit visual stress when she was studying. She would take regular breaks during which she would gaze out her window at the buildings across the street. She discovered that these breaks did not hinder but actually helped her learning. Shifting the focus of her attention gave her a wider perspective on her work. By looking up from the single tree on the page before her, she was able while gazing away to see the forest of the subject she was engaged in.

In time Julie O. got her doctor's degree and went into practice as a family therapist.

•

The video display terminal magnifies and multiplies the visual problems of desk work. The machines themselves are multiplying: the number of VDTs in use is expected to increase from fifteen million in 1988 to seventy million in 1990. As the number of people working at these machines grows, so does the number among them who complain of visual difficulties, and they complain at a greater rate than their counterparts who are working with paper.

The VDT is not just another form of reading. Electronic and printed images differ in quality. A given sentence is harder to read on the VDT than on the printed page. Whereas the printed copy is clear and still, the video image is comparatively blurred and is constantly moving and flickering. Dr. Lawrence Stark, a neurologist member of a National Academy of Science committee on the impact of video display, said: "VDTs require much more of the visual system than any other office-related visual tasks. . . . VDT characters are not as readable as printed material." The VDT has also made visual work more concentrated by changing the way many jobs are performed. The more steps of the job that can be performed on the VDT, the less respite the operator gets from staring at the terminal. The order-entry clerk is an example. Before computers, he would take orders by telephone, then write them up by hand or typewriter on an order form. He often had to carry papers to other desks or offices. Thus he had frequent cause to interrupt his close visual work. Not with the VDT. That same clerk wears a phone headset and enters all his information directly into the terminal. His work provides him few if any visual breaks.

In our practice we are seeing a fast-growing number of patients who spend their working days in front of a VDT. Their complaints fall into patterns. Their sight blurs, they see double, they have trouble changing focus when they look away from the screen. Their eyes burn and ache. They feel eyestrain and visual fatigue. They have frequent headaches, especially of the forehead.

Certainly, as we have seen, these same complaints have often been voiced by desk workers who use paper only. But the complaints seem to us more prevalent and more severe among VDT operators. Some patients have told us they had no trouble with desk work until they started using the VDT. Our impression that the VDT causes added complaints is borne out by statistics. Several studies have shown a much higher rate of visual complaints among VDT operators than among other desk workers. One study compared the rate of complaint in five categories:

COMPLAINT	percent VDT workers	percent non-VDT clerical workers
CHANGE IN COLOR PERCEPTION	40	9
IRRITATED EYES	74	47
BURNING EYES	80	44
BLURRED VISION	71	35
EYESTRAIN	91	60

Patients tell us their visual problems have a direct and harmful effect on their work and on their general health. They cannot work as fast or as well or get as much done in a day. They make more errors in transcribing words and numbers, more reversals, omissions, substitutions. Visual fatigue leads to physical fatigue, visual stress to overall stress. They are more susceptible to illness: virus, colds, allergies.

And—employers, take note—our patients lose more days out sick. Many corporate managers have instituted wellness programs for their employees in the belief that better employee health means a healthier balance sheet. We believe that employers with any kind of desk workers, but most especially VDT operators, would be well advised to include vision in their wellness programs. Such a program would include regular examinations—not merely the standard Snellen chart but the full range of visual skills—and vision therapy where indicated. The figures on the effects of close work on employees persuade us that such a program would easily pay for itself in improved productivity and reduced absenteeism.

Again, statistics confirm what we observe among our patients. An Air Force study of office automation found a high degree of complaints such as head- and backaches, even arm and leg pains, along with directly visual complaints such as eyestrain. A survey of eleven hundred members of the Newspaper Guild found that "more VDT users than non-users said they had been absent from work three or more times in the preceding two years." An eye clinic specializing in VDT operators—the Video Display Terminal Eye Clinic in Berkeley, California—has found that an unusually large number of its patients have trouble focusing their eyes.

Much of the human discomfort and suffering these statistics represent is unnecessary. There are ways to reduce the visual and physical impact of the VDT. These fall into two categories: improving the conditions in which VDT operators work, and helping the operators improve their visual skills so they can better handle the burden of the machine.

Most VDT operators work in circumstances that fall far short of the ideal. Proper conditions begin with the right arrangement of the operator in relation to the machine. The diagram on p. 100 shows a well-designed workstation. The chair supports the back and is adjustable so the operator can keep both feet flat on the floor. The seat pad is set so that the person's legs are 1 or 2 inches from the chair with his back against the backrest. The forearms and wrists are approximately horizontal while using the keyboard. The display screen is above the keyboard, about arm's length (18–20 inches) from the operator's eyes, and 20–30 degrees below his direct line of sight. (Why below rather than straight ahead? As in so many aspects of vision, the answer goes back to our remote ancestors. When they were working with their hands, whether cracking nuts or tearing meat from the carcass, they too were looking down rather than straight ahead.)

Glare and reflection must be minimized. Ideally, the display screen

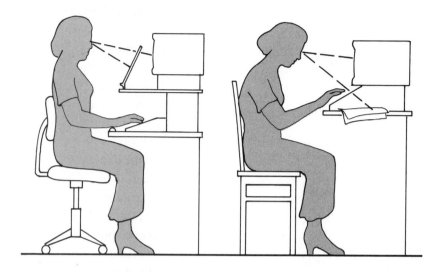

VIDEO DISPLAY TERMINAL WORKSTATIONS

Note the contrasts between the well-designed station, left, and one that is poorly designed. At left, the chair provides support for the back and its height is adjustable so that the operator can maintain good posture and can keep her feet flat on the floor. Both the video screen and the document to the right of the screen are at about a forearm's length from the eyes and about 20–30 degrees below eye level. The height of the adjustable table is set so that the operator's forearms and wrists are approximately horizontal while using the keyboard, and so her legs clear the underside of the table.

should have a neutral matte finish. A filter can also be put over the screen. Operators should avoid wearing light-colored clothes, which, combined with the light given off by the screen, cause both glare and reflection.

Resolution, the visual quality of the display on the screen, is determined by the density of the phosphorescent dots, called pixels, which when electronically excited form the images we see. (The same is true of a television screen.) The higher the resolution—that is, the greater the concentration of pixels—the better it is for the eyes. "Swim" (the slight waving motion of the image) and on-off flickering are subtly harmful to the eyes. Both can be minimized by getting a machine of good quality and then making sure it is well maintained.

The thinking about the right colors on the screen has changed since the early days of computers. The makers of the first screens used the familiar black and white. This provided good contrast, as it does on paper, but on the VDT the combination was fatiguing to the eyes. A green background with either black or white letters is now considered best. Green lies halfway between red and blue on the spectrum of visible light and is the color to which our eyes are most sensitive.

Lighting requirements change when work moves from paper to the VDT. Because the terminal itself is lit, a VDT operator needs only half the lighting needed by someone working with paper. What used to be the right amount of illumination in the room is likely now to be too much. Because today's screen is higher in relation to our eyes than yesterday's paper, overhead glare will be more bothersome. Diffuse, indirect lighting is preferable. Fluorescent lights provide this, but, for reasons of eye health having nothing to do with the VDT, they should be the full-spectrum kind. (See Appendix A for more on lighting.) Windows are valuable as a source of visual relief, but can cause glare if their light falls directly on the workstation.

People who work on the VDT must have ample and frequent opportunity to take breaks from the near-point visual concentration of their work. Ideally, they should have five to ten minutes every hour away from the machine. That time away from the terminal should not be spent in any other kind of close visual activity such as reading a newspaper or even glancing through a magazine. The purpose of the break is to give workers a chance to cast their eyes off into the distance, and so there must be an opportunity for that distant view. Even a brief glance far away from the terminal helps reduce the strain on the eyes. That is why windows are valuable.

That essential distant view is denied by those employers who, in order to save space, put banks of VDT operators in tiny cubicles where their visual space is as little as 4 feet. The person working in that cubicle has no relief from the stress of his close work on the terminal. The result is disastrous. Whatever else is being produced in those cubicles, one product is certain: nearsightedness. As we point out in Chapter 10, such a setting is a breeding ground for myopia. Here in that cubicle is where we are likely to find the person whose myopia leveled off in his early twenties and now in his thirties is suddenly getting worse again. Here, too, we will find the person who is becoming nearsighted for the first time.

Employers may save money on the rent by herding their VDT

workers into those visual sweatshops, but they will pay a high price in lower productivity on the job and more days out sick. It is likely, in our view, that the employer would be better off paying more rent in order to get more production from healthier, happier workers. For the employees themselves, there is no doubt they would be better off, much better off, out of the cubicles.

Only so much can be done by improving the work environment. A comparison of the rates of vision problems under best and worst conditions suggests that the best environment will reduce complaints by at most 39 percent. Better resolution on the screen, even if it is improved to the quality of paper, can reduce complaints by only 11 percent. Most VDT problems are due to the visual limitations of the operators themselves and must be resolved with glasses or vision therapy or a combination of the two.

People who already wear glasses are very likely to need a new prescription when they go to work on a VDT. The usual prescription, intended to provide 20/20 sight on the chart, is often poorly adapted to the VDT. This is particularly true of the middle-aged person who wears bifocals. Because the display screen is both higher and farther away, he cannot read as he normally would with his bifocals. He has to tilt his head back to look at the screen through his lower lenses. Pretty soon his neck is aching. His situation and that of other wearers of glasses can be remedied with special glasses for the VDT. In recent years lenses have been developed, often with a single or variable focus, that can be tailored to the specific needs of the job. Anyone who already wears glasses and is starting on the VDT is well advised to ask his eye doctor for work glasses and to give the doctor the most precise description he can of the visual requirements of his job, especially the exact distance between his eyes and the screen.

Once more, research confirms the observations we have made in our practice. Two eye doctors at the State College of Optometry in New York, Barry J. Barresi and Jesse Rosenthal, reported on 775 VDT workers who were given special eye tests by a panel of optometrists. Three-quarters were given glasses tailored to their jobs. Among those who answered a follow-up questionnaire, 94 percent reported greater comfort and 82 percent said the quality and efficiency of their work had improved. "The benefit seems to be most effective for the worker who is over forty years old and is already wearing a vision correction [glasses or contacts] at work," the researchers observed.

The VDT is far more demanding of visual skills than other kinds of desk work. It requires high performance in eye movements, in binocular vision, and in the ability to focus for long stretches and then change focus without blurring. If a person's skills in these areas are mediocre, he will experience discomfort working for any length of time on the VDT, and if his skills are poor his handicap will be severe. Vision therapy will bring this person's skills up to the point where, given good working conditions, he can do a day's work on the machine without discomfort. Vision therapy can also enhance skills that are already good. For the person whose skills are good enough for most daily uses, therapy can raise the level of those skills so that he can work the VDT with greater ease and efficiency. He will be able to do more and better work and feel better while he is doing it.

●

JEAN A. is a computer programmer in her late twenties. Her work is very demanding on her vision. She spends 80 percent of her working day looking at the VDT screen, and the rest of her day is devoted to close desk work.

She was referred to us by her eye doctor. She told us that her eyes were tiring, she was seeing double, she was missing whole paragraphs when she read, she was suffering from frequent headaches. She also mentioned that she had been operated on at age thirteen for an eye that turned out.

We found that the surgery had overcorrected the eye so that instead of turning out it now turned in. The brain was intermittently suppressing the messages from that eye; when it accepted those messages, Jean was seeing double. We suggested a course of therapy and prescribed work glasses that include a prism to help hold her eye in line and are coated to screen out ultraviolet radiation.

Now, after a year of therapy, plus eight weeks of reinforcement two years later, Jean A. finds that her vision is much improved. Her turned eye is straight, and she no longer sees double or suppresses one eye. She has no trouble with close work. She no longer has headaches or misses paragraphs. Most important, she can do a day's work at the VDT without the trouble she used to have. She also has made it a habit to take regular breaks, every forty-five minutes or so, to relieve the visual concentration of her work. She has enough visual energy left over to be able to read at home in the evening.

•

VINCENT L. is an electronics technician. He repairs computer-related equipment of various sorts. Some of his tasks involve intricate work with tiny wires calling for good eye-hand coordination. But most of his day is spent either staring into the VDT screen or reading small type in thick manuals.

When he was thirty Vincent L. began to feel very uncomfortable in his work. Reading the manuals was especially frustrating. He could not get through the instructions at one sitting. He would read a page, then feel he had to stop and get up. He was beginning to guess at the instructions or rely on what he had heard—anything to avoid reading the manual. He got a headache at the prospect of paper work. He had trouble judging where things were in space. Reading had always made him uncomfortable. Never a good reader or speller, he had gotten through high school by listening carefully. Later his poor reading had caused him to drop out of one school after another. Now he was unpleasantly aware of a disparity between what he produced and the work of others. He wasn't working up to his ability and he knew it. He tried glasses, but this, he said, was "worse than nothing." Then he was referred to us.

When we examined Vincent we found he suffered from convergence insufficiency: he found it difficult to align his eyes on a close target and hold them there. His visual skills were those of a fourth-grader. We gave him a reading-comprehension test, in which, in his own words, he "did pretty horribly." We proposed therapy to improve his visual skills. We also prescribed glasses that corrected his farsightedness and astigmatism without causing discomfort.

Vincent's therapy lasted nine months. It was a complete success. His eyes now work together without difficulty. His life is greatly improved, both at work and at home. He no longer has trouble reading long reports, and he suffers no headaches or frustration in front of the VDT. His work is much better. In fact, he has been promoted twice. His reading comprehension tests far higher than it did when he started with us: he has gone from fourth grade to college level in less than a year. He reads 325 words a minute where he used to read no more than 110. Still a poor speller, he now is willing to look a word up and get it right. He is even, for the first time in his life, reading for pleasure. He reads spy stories passed on to him by his wife.

●

One subtle visual skill deserves separate mention. This is the balance between central and peripheral vision, between what we see where we focus our eyes and what we are aware of in the larger surrounding area. (See p. 142 for a discussion of this skill in athletes.) If this relationship is properly balanced, the person at the VDT or doing any other close work will be able to center his primary attention on his work while maintaining a good sense of where he is in his environment. He will be aware of what is going on around him but not distracted by it. (This, too, we owe to our ancestors, whose peripheral vision warned them of impending danger while they focused on the immediate tasks of cracking those nuts or tearing that meat.) If the person's attention is too peripheral he will be easily distracted by movements or sounds around him. If, on the other hand, he is over-balanced toward the center, he will be able to concentrate but he will also be easily fatigued.

Therapeutic exercises improve the visual balance between central and peripheral awareness. A better balance in our perception has an analogy in our mental performance. At the center our mind is focused on the most immediate part of the task, while on the periphery of the mind we are aware of the larger aspects of our work. At the center, our attention is on the present—what we are doing right now. On the periphery, we are aware of past and future—what we have just done and what we are going to do next. Here, too, a better balance between the two will improve human performance, not just on the VDT but in many aspects of life.

Such are the ways in which the harmful impact of this new technology can be prevented or at least softened. Needless perhaps to say, current practice is far from perfect. We are seeing efforts for change, as in the 1988 passage of legislation in Suffolk County, New York, requiring employers to provide regular breaks and treatment for the damage their machines do to their employees' eyes. Yet few VDT operators work under anything close to the best conditions as we have described them, and fewer still have adequate access to the glasses and therapy they may need.

The problem will not go away. In a world ever more dependent on computers, the VDT and the damage it can do will be with us for the foreseeable future. We have to learn to live with it. Tarzan (more often it's Jane) will still be sitting in front of that terminal. But he—and she—need not suffer as they do today. They need not and they should not.

7

DRIVING AND
HOUSEHOLD ACCIDENTS

Driving is one modern activity for which our ancestors were in many ways visually well prepared. In most of this book we have been discussing visual skills needed for close work, skills for which the eyes we inherited from our forebears are poorly adapted. Driving, by contrast, calls on the same skills that our ancestors needed in order to find their food and at the same time escape becoming a meal for a hungry predator.

•

PETER B. was one of our most unusual and challenging cases. Most patients come to us with more or less severe visual problems. Not Peter B. His vision was excellent, his visual skills far above average. The challenge he posed was to make his excellent skills even better.

Peter B., who is in his thirties, is a serious amateur race-car driver. Almost any weekend from spring through fall finds him out on one track or another racing against his peers. He has never had serious problems with his eyes. In graduate school, when he was reading six to eight hours a day, he'd notice his sight blurring occasionally. He got reading glasses, but hasn't worn them since graduation because his profession does not require concentrated close work. On the racetrack, however, Peter B. is an intense competitor. He'd heard of vision therapy and wondered if it could improve his vision and thereby his racing. "It wasn't enough for my vision to work right," he said later. "I wanted it to work just right. I wanted the last one percent."

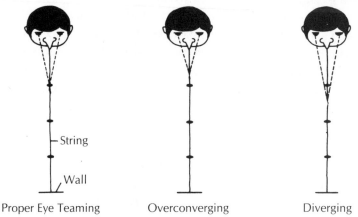

Proper Eye Teaming   Overconverging   Diverging

WHERE THE EYES REALLY FOCUS

Testing with the "Brock String" reveals whether the eyes actually converge on the intended target. The patient holds the string as shown in the photo and is asked to focus on the bead closest to her. The string will appear to her as two converging lines. As seen in the diagram, the lines may appear to meet in front of the bead if the patient's eyes are overconverging. She will see things as being somewhat closer than they really are—and will respond according to that perception. If the lines seem to meet beyond the bead, the eyes are diverging and the patient will see things as farther away than they are. If the patient is asked to reach out and touch the bead, she will touch the string in front of the bead if her eyes overconverge, beyond it if they diverge. The judgment of distance tested by the Brock String is important in driving and in many sports.·

We examined Peter B. and found that, excellent as his skills were, some aspects of his vision were less than perfect. The Brock String tests spatial judgment: the patient reaches out to touch a point on a string that the therapist holds perpendicular to his eyes. Peter B. would reach slightly beyond the actual location of the point. He was seeing things—like other race cars —somewhat further away than they really were, and so he was reacting a split second late. When his eyes tired, as they would late in a long race, he would have trouble refocusing and would lose a little of his intense concentration. We told him we could try to help him to gain that last 1 percent of his vision. Peter B. entered a course of therapy in which we concentrated on those few skills that could be improved. He came to us two hours a week for four months. Of his therapy, he recalled particularly an exercise in which he drew lines with each hand simultaneously while seeing the lines he was reproducing separately with each of his eyes. "I knew that the closer the lines came together the closer I was to seeing what's actually out there," he said.

Peter B. reported "a noticeable improvement in my visual perception" after his therapy. For him, what mattered about his therapy—all that mattered—was what happened out on the track, and that was where he saw the difference. In his first race after therapy, he sensed an obvious improvement in his ability to concentrate visually: "I didn't have the feeling of losing concentration midway in the race." Three weeks later, racing on an unusually fast track, Peter B. had "a distinct impression that things were slowing down, that I had more time to react. Not much, but in a race it doesn't take much to make the difference." This is a familiar phenomenon. Many an athlete has told us after vision therapy that things—a ball he is trying to hit, for example —seem to be moving slower. Of course the ball, or in Peter B.'s case another car, is not in fact moving with any less speed. But his visual system is moving faster. It is processing information and presenting it to the brain more rapidly, and this gives the athlete an extra moment to respond. As any athlete will say, a moment—even a split second—may be all it takes.

The next weekend Peter B. thought he was driving very well in the first day's race. The next day he spent the first fourteen laps "chasing somebody." He experienced no loss of concentration. "I was giving it one hundred percent all the way," he recalled. "I sensed the moment when he was losing his visual concentration, and I caught him on the next to last lap!" He explained to us that in that moment he had hurdled a psychological barrier in racing. "Usually if you try to pass a car for several laps and fail, something inside says you can't do it; you slow down and then you'll never catch him," he said. "This time that didn't happen to me."

•

For his kind of driving Peter B. obviously needs visual skills well beyond those required by most of us as we plod along the highway. Yet even everyday driving demands a high degree of visual skill, especially in those moments of emergency that any driver must sooner or later meet. The frightening reality is that a large proportion of people licensed to drive lack those skills. The evidence is in the great number of accidents after which the driver will say something like: "I didn't see that car coming" or "I looked but I didn't see it."

Driving requires much more than good sight. What matters, after all, is not just what the driver sees but what he does with what he sees and when he does it. Thus, in addition to visual skills, he needs good visual perception to interpret what his eyes see, the ability to react in time, and good eye-hand and eye-foot coordination to carry out effectively what he's decided to do.

Unfortunately, hardly any of these skills are tested by the state authorities who issue driver's licenses. For those few skills that are tested, the standards are usually too low: too low even for ordinary drivers, and, in our opinion, far too low for those like bus and truck drivers who carry extra responsibilities.

Visual acuity at distance—the familiar chart on the wall—is the only skill that is universally tested. The usual requirement for an ordinary license is 20/40 with glasses (sometimes this applies only to one eye). Some states set a higher minimum for bus or truck licenses.

Acuity of 20/40 is truly a minimal requirement, adequate if at all only for ordinary driving by daylight. At least two studies have shown that drivers with relatively poor acuity have a greater rate of accidents. At night the difference becomes much greater. According to one authority, optometrist Merrill J. Allen, author of the landmark study *Vision and Highway Safety*, that driver with 20/40 by daylight may after dark have effective sight of only 20/200: far too poor for safety.

The usual test is for static acuity—how well we see when neither we nor the object we look at is in motion. But obviously, in driving, both the driver and other cars are in motion. As we say in more detail in Chapter 9, dynamic acuity does not follow from static acuity. Unfortunately, only a handful of states test for this important skill.

Visual acuity is just the beginning of a driver's visual needs. It measures only our ability to see what we are looking at. Usually that is what is in front of us. But most highway emergencies come at us from where we are not looking. That is what makes them emergencies. Avoiding the possible accident calls on our peripheral vision, the ability to sense an unusual motion off to the side, out of the corner of the eye, just as our ancestors sensed that saber-toothed tiger creeping up on them. Peripheral vision gives us a warning to turn our eyes and identify a possible danger.

A person with normal peripheral vision has a visual field of about 180 degrees, which means he is able to detect movement at a right angle on either side while he is focusing straight ahead. (You can test your own peripheral vision by holding your arms out to each side and wiggling your hands while looking straight ahead at a fixed target. See how far back you can move your hands before they vanish from sight.) A visual field of less than 180 degrees is abnormal, and less than 140 degrees is hazardous. A crucial fact here is that effective peripheral vision decreases with speed because stationary objects go by too fast to register on our eyes. Thus a visual field of 180 degrees when standing still shrinks to 104 degrees at 20 miles per hour and to 42 degrees at 60 miles per hour. The driver going 60 has lost three-quarters of his peripheral vision. (See illustration on page 112.)

Again, peripheral vision bears no relation to visual acuity. Yet few states test for it, and those few require only 140 degrees even for bus or truck licenses.

Depth perception is another essential skill that is seldom tested. This is how we judge the distance between, say, ourselves and another car, and act accordingly. Ideally, we judge distance with the help of binocular vision: the two eyes seeing the same object at

Full Field—standing still

20 miles per hour

HOW SPEED DIMINISHES VISION

Peripheral vision, which extends almost to 180 degrees when the person is motionless, decreases dramatically with increasing speed. At 20 miles an hour, a driver's peripheral vision is only 104 degrees, and at 60, he can see only 42 degrees—less than one-fourth his peripheral vision at rest. Note that the car at right has disappeared completely from the driver's awareness when he is going 60. He will get no warning of the car's presence until it is almost directly in front of him.

60 miles per hour

slightly different angles give us an immediate sense of three-dimensional space. People who lack binocular vision must judge distance by using clues from other sources—for example, the space visible between two moving cars. Experience can make up for much that would otherwise come from binocularity, though probably with a loss in reaction time. The most obvious instance of a lack of binocularity is a one-eyed person, but many others also fall into this category. People with poor muscular control of their eyes find it hard to hold binocular vision. When they are tired, they may see double. When driving they can usually manage in daylight, though at some cost in fatigue and discomfort. At night, however, their vision may become unmanageable, especially under the added influence of alcohol, drugs (including medication), or exhaust fumes.

People with a turned eye (strabismus) or lazy eye (amblyopia) may have sight in both eyes but lack effective binocular vision. In *Vision and Highway Safety*, Merrill Allen identifies the person operated on for strabismus as a particular highway risk because he is likely to be less well adapted to his handicap than he was before the surgery. "Unfortunately the more hazardous surgically treated group will not be obvious to the motor vehicle examiner, while the probably safe untreated squinter will be easy to detect," he writes. Allen believes that this surgically treated driver "should be restricted to daytime low-stress situations," whereas a turned eye "cured by non-surgical means can be considered normal."

Farsightedness is never tested, but in Allen's opinion it can be dangerous. In *Vision and Highway Safety* he wrote: "I believe that a large proportion of one-car accidents late at night result from misjudgments by young drivers who have 0.75 diopter or more of uncorrected hyperopia [a moderate degree of farsightedness] and who are fatigued. Upon loss of the bright lights of other cars, as happens late at night, they may lose control of fusion [the ability to keep both eyes aimed at a single object], become confused or frightened, and run off the road. Such youngsters typically have 20/20 vision or better in the daytime."

Color perception is another important visual skill that is not tested as it should be—only seven states currently do so. A substantial number of people (8 percent of men, 0.5 percent of women) are deficient in their ability to distinguish color. Color-deficient people have a higher rate of error while driving because the extra effort they must make to distinguish color tends to distract their attention from other aspects of driving. If their deficiency is in red and green, they will take twice as long to react to a traffic signal. Other visually related skills that are not tested are adaptability to darkness and resistance to glare (both of which diminish with age).

Visual reaction time is perhaps the most dangerous among the many omissions in our present testing of would-be drivers. How quickly we are able to react is after all what determines how well we use all our other visual skills. Time is always short in a highway emergency, and it is no use seeing the emergency if we cannot react fast enough to avoid the accident. People in fact vary greatly in their reaction time, and they do so independently of their other visual skills. Knowing that a person has excellent acuity, for example, tells us nothing about that person's ability to react to what he sees. What makes this omission most unfortunate is that reaction time is easily tested and easily improved. Almost anyone with a little training can reduce his reaction time—enough perhaps one day to make the difference between life and death.

From this review of the complex mix of visual skills we need in order to drive safely, it is obvious that well-informed licensing authorities intent on reducing the toll of highway accidents would set far higher standards for the licenses they issue. We believe that states should appoint commissions that include vision experts to set new and far higher standards not only for licensing but for driver education. Student drivers especially should—in addition to being tested for all the visual skills, including reaction time and peripheral vision —be offered an opportunity to bring their skills up to the minimum standard. No student should be licensed who lacks the necessary skills, but every student should be given access to acquiring those skills. All candidate drivers should be given that same opportunity, of course, but it is particularly easy to achieve in a school setting. We believe that making sure that all who drive have the visual skills the job requires would save at least as many lives as reducing speed limits from 70 to 55 miles per hour; the driver with poor skills is at least as dangerous at 55 as is the driver with good skills at 70.

We are aware that setting the safest standards is politically difficult. Most Americans, and particularly those who are young and male, consider a license to drive as part of their birthright. In a more practical vein, we live in a society in which the automobile is an essential part of our lives. For many of us it is the only way we can get to work and get to the store. These rights must be balanced against the ideal of safety.

Still, much could be done within those limits. Minimum standards should certainly be set higher than they are today. An essential first step would be to test the full range of visual skills of all applicants for any sort of driver's license. This need not be difficult: a layman using a simple kit could test the essential skills in less than four minutes. The results of that test would form part of the driver's record and might indeed be attached to the license. Drivers' vision should be retested at regular intervals, more often when they are elderly and skills may be diminishing, and should also be retested after any accident in which their vision might be a factor. Insurance companies might be persuaded to set different rates for different levels of skill as they do today for different age groups.

Most important, people who meet the minimum and yet are visually deficient should be restricted to daytime driving. There might well be a separate test for night driving. As we have seen, visual deficiencies that are acceptable in daylight become intolerably dangerous after dark. To allow such people to drive by night is unfair not only to others but even to themselves. Restricting them to daytime is a sensible compromise between the interests of safety and the rights of the individual. Daytime, after all, is sufficient for most people to get to work and for everyone to get to the store.

The case with those who drive trucks, buses, and taxis is different. Buses and taxis carry human cargo in addition to their drivers, and buses and trucks by their very size are dangerous. Truck, bus, and taxi drivers spend more time on the road and so put the rest of us more at risk. The individual's right to drive does not apply here any more than it does to the would-be airline pilot who cannot pass the eye exam. In the interest of the great majority, applicants for these licenses should be held to high standards for the full range of visual skills. That means much higher standards than are applied today.

No doubt it will be a long time before such reforms are put into practice. In the meantime there is much the individual driver can do. He can begin with the awareness that he shares the road with a great many drivers whose visual skills are deficient and that he himself may be among them. If he has any reason to suspect that he belongs in that category—an accident or near-miss in which "I didn't see that car coming" is an excellent reason—he should find an eye doctor who can check the full range of his visual skills. If he finds his vision wanting, he should consider restricting himself to low-stress daytime driving—or even take himself off the road entirely. As the old saying goes, the life he saves may be his own.

Many visual skills can be improved by conscientious practice while driving. Peter B., in an interview after his vision therapy, suggested a variety of ways in which the average driver can practice his skills and thereby prepare himself better to cope with emergency.

Avoid staring. Drivers who keep their eyes on the car in front, as if they were staring at a television screen, lose a large part of their visual field. Keep the eyes in motion. Practice rapid changes in the distance of focus—for example, switching focus from the car in front to the road far ahead and to the rearview mirror. The faster the better. The more the eyes are in motion, the better is the driver's awareness of where his vehicle is in relation to others. The less he stares, the better his peripheral vision.

Practice using the rearview mirrors, bearing in mind that distance and size are distorted in the mirrors. Try while looking at the road ahead to watch the mirrors with the "soft focus" of peripheral vision. A driver who cautiously plays learning games with the mirrors while driving—judging the distance and speed of cars, for example—is actually practicing how to reduce his reaction time; and that moment which he learns to save by practice may prove to be a livesaver in an emergency.

To use the mirrors most effectively the driver must keep a constant position in his seat so that he can find each mirror without having to look around for it. If he is slouched to one side, he will miss the mirror on first glance. This, Peter B. believes, is the primary purpose of the seat belt, to keep the driver positioned at right angles to the wheel so that he knows, without looking, where to find the mirrors.

Getting around the house may not seem to call for the visual skills involved in driving or the close visual work of an accountant or a dentist. But the person managing a household must carry out a wide variety of tasks that call for a variety of visual skills, and the lack of those skills spells trouble. Each year many thousands of people in the United States are injured in household accidents. Most of those accidents have a visual aspect that, if corrected, would have prevented them from happening. We tend to blame accidents on "clumsiness" and shrug them off as inevitable: that's the way the person is. But clumsiness in most cases simply means poor eye-hand coordination, and that can be improved with vision therapy.

A person with a severe visual problem can find the daily routines of life intolerably difficult. Such was the situation of Libby K.:

●

LIBBY K.'s vision was in bad shape when she came to us. It was so bad, in fact, that we wondered how she could get around at all. From what she told us about her life it was clear that just getting around was indeed very hard for her.

Libby K. had had trouble with her vision as a child. She was always jittery when she had to study. She jumped around while she was reading. An eye doctor gave her a magnifying lens, which helped a little. Because she was unusually intelligent, she was able to get through high school despite her poor reading, though she recalls she was always nervous during tests. At college she majored in music and dance. She loved to dance, but she also chose it to minimize the reading she would have to do.

Later she was married and had two children. She ran a dance program for young children. With no schoolwork to do, she was more or less free of visual problems for many years.

When, however, she reached her mid-forties, Libby K.'s vision suddenly became much worse. Her ability to compensate for visual defects began to deteriorate rapidly. The actions of daily life that she had taken for granted became nearly impossible. "I was virtually nonfunctional," she recalled. "I was seeing double. My eyes were jumping all around." She could read hardly at all, and then only by using a ruler to follow the lines. She had enjoyed knitting; now she could no longer knit or thread a needle. She bumped her head into kitchen cabinets. Driving became hazardous. When she backed her car out she would suddenly lose her sight and run off the driveway. She couldn't stand to look at a patterned rug. Libby K. even had to give up the dancing that she loved. Her balance was so bad she could not turn or jump without falling down. She was afraid to take off her glasses without closing her eyes because that meant seeing double. "I was always complaining," she said. "So many little things went wrong." She was nervous, high-strung, unhappy.

We found that Libby K. suffered from strabismus. Her right eye tended to turn in, and there was also a vertical imbalance between the two eyes. We started her on an intensive course of vision therapy: twice a week for five months. After her therapy Libby K.'s vision was much improved. Her eye no longer appeared to turn. Her life was also much improved. She began to read again. "It's still not easy," she said. "But I can read short articles in the paper." She no longer bumps her head into kitchen cabinets. She can drive without running off the driveway or hitting the curb. Most important, she has started dancing again. When she is tired her vision may falter and she has to stop and rest her eyes. But she feels she is far better off than she was. Daily life is no longer traumatic. "My husband notices the change in me," she said. "I'm much more relaxed these days. And I can dance."

•

8

THE LATER YEARS
AND LOW VISION

Too many older people give up too soon and too easily. Because of a visual problem, they give up on activities that mean a great deal in their lives. Often these are the pleasures they had looked forward to enjoying in retirement. All the books they'd planned to read—but now it hurts their eyes to read more than a few pages. All the long, leisurely trips by car—but now they're afraid to drive because they can't see well enough and their responses are too slow. The afternoons on the golf course or the tennis court once office days were over—but now they can't see the ball properly to hit it.

Many give up their cherished independence and move into a retirement home of some sort. When residents of a continuing-care residence in Pennsylvania were surveyed, failure of vision was the most frequently given reason for leaving their homes. The eyes lead the body, and because their eyes were failing them they thought they could no longer cope.

The tragedy is that in so many cases they give up unnecessarily.

Usually these older people have taken their problems to an eye doctor and found out that their prescription is correct and their eyes show no signs of disease; and they say that nonetheless their eyes are bothering them. All too often the eye doctor replies with something like: "It can't be helped. It's part of growing old."

The second statement is correct. It is indeed part of growing old.

The first statement is demonstrably false. It is disproved every day by those older people who are seeking and getting help for the visual problems that come with aging. Unfortunately those who seek help are a small minority of those who need it.

The statistics are convincing. The most common visual problem of older people can be treated, in an otherwise healthy patient, with a success rate of better than 90 percent. That has been the experience in our practice. It is also what other eye doctors report who offer vision therapy for the elderly.

After vision therapy, the overwhelming majority of our patients can read comfortably for long stretches of time, can see to drive safely, can go on playing golf or tennis. If they have to give up any of these activities, it will not be because of their vision.

But for every patient treated successfully with vision therapy, there are many others who go untreated. These unfortunate older people find their lives diminished and themselves put on the shelf before their time. All because they were told that "It can't be helped. It's part of growing old."

Our eyes do grow old as our bodies age. Along with strictly medical problems, which may or may not be curable, there is a set of visual disorders which commonly afflict older people. Among their common complaints are the following:

Visually intense close work is hard to do and especially hard to sustain. They can no longer thread a needle. Many say they can no longer read for any length of time. Their eyes tire and get sore, their sight blurs, and they see double. Reading gives them headaches. They skip words, can't follow what they're reading, forget what they just read. They fall asleep over a book even in the morning when they're well rested. The housewife who used to shop from memory finds that when she is in the store she can no longer remember what she saw when she looked around the kitchen to find out what she needed.

People suddenly become clumsy. They drop dishes, bump into the furniture. When walking, they stumble and sometimes fall, and that fall may break a limb. Such a fall is potentially much more serious for them than it used to be, for a fracture that healed in a few weeks when they were in their twenties may take a year or more when they are decades older.

Seeing in shadowed areas is harder now. So is seeing when they enter sudden darkness: it takes longer to find a vacant seat at the movies.

Searching with the eyes no longer works as it once did. Especially in an unfamiliar place, it's harder to locate and identify street signs, house numbers, a bus stop.

Driving becomes chancy. The driver sees less well out of the corner of his eyes, and so he may not notice a car coming at him from the side. His effective peripheral vision has diminished. He may still test adequately, but when his attention is divided, as it is while driving, the peripheral system won't work as it once did.

Driving in the uncertain light of sunset—difficult even for young eyes—becomes even more so for older ones. And, as one older person who is himself an optometrist observed, twilight seems to come earlier than it used to.

The older person's visual reaction time—his ability to respond promptly to what he sees—is slower. This is obviously a critical problem when he is driving.

Traveling the roads of an area with a large geriatric population will highlight the troubles of older drivers. Driving in parts of South Florida, for example, is something like crossing a minefield. Here you routinely see cars creeping along a highway at dangerously low speeds and suddenly making left turns from the far-right lane. You see also that the car is essential to the lives of many older people. It is the only way they can get out, can get to the store or visit someone; without the car they cannot maintain their independence. (In Chapter 7 we argue for much more extensive visual testing of applicants for licenses and for more frequent retesting of older drivers. Those measures, if adopted, would undoubtedly result in removing the licenses of some older people. But a much larger number could learn to drive as safely as they once did if their visual problems were resolved.)

Finally, the aging amateur athlete finds that something has gone wrong. He may say that "my timing is all off now." He can't see to hit the ball properly because he can no longer judge accurately where the ball is.

Such are the major symptoms that older people report, the visual problems that cause so many of them to give up activities for which they are otherwise fit, and for which, with help, most of them could again be visually fit.

From our clinical point of view, overwhelmingly their most common visual disorder is what we call "convergence insufficiency." It is no exaggeration to say that this disorder reaches epidemic proportions among older people. Its cause lies in the effect of aging on a very subtle aspect of the human visual system.

When we decide to look at something, the brain issues two sets of orders along two separate nervous systems. The voluntary nervous system orders the muscles that move the eyeball to align the eyes— to pull the eyes together so that both are fixed on the target. That is convergence. ("Divergence" is asking the eyes to align on a target more distant than the one on which they are now aligned.) At the same time the involuntary nervous system orders the lens of the eye to focus on the target. This takes the form of an order to the ciliary muscle, located in the eye itself, to change the shape of the lens so that it will cast a clear image on the retina. But—and this is the key to the problem—this second set of orders also spills over to the convergence system as a reinforcing order to the eye muscles. This spillover command is necessary to the successful working of convergence, of pulling in and holding our eyes on the target.

Over a life-span the lens gradually stiffens. As it loses its flexibility, the ciliary muscle is no longer able to bring the lens into the shape needed to focus accurately. The stiffening starts as early as our teens but usually does not become apparent until around age forty. That is when we find we no longer can see clearly up close, notably when we are reading. This is when the nearsighted person, who already needs one correction for distance, finds he needs a different correction to see close up. So he starts wearing bifocals.

With the decline in the ability of the lens to focus comes a corresponding decline in the spillover effect, the reinforcing order to the eye muscles to align the eyes on the target. Now the convergence system begins to break down because it cannot do its job without the reinforcing command. (As is usually the case in disorders of vision, there is nothing wrong with the eye muscles themselves; they are just not getting the right commands.)

As a result, the eyes cannot align themselves properly and they cannot sustain alignment, particularly when doing close work. That is why the older person cannot read comfortably for any length of time. (Convergence insufficiency also occurs among the young, notably among school-age children who have trouble reading, but only later in life is it an epidemic.) It is also why older people have trouble judging the distance of a moving object. Our perception of that object depends in part on the contrast between clear and blurred images as it moves in and out of focus. The loss of that contrast, as a result of diminished ability to focus and convergence insufficiency, makes it hard to tell just where that moving object is, whether it be another car or a tennis ball.

The method of treating convergence insufficiency is well known to those of us who offer vision therapy. We first administer a series of diagnostic tests that measure the specifics of the problem. We then start the patient on a course of vision therapy targeted to those specifics. Typically this will include routines in which each eye works alone, in order to equalize their skills; routines in which the two eyes work at the same time but separately, which will eliminate the common problem of the brain rejecting the messages of one eye; and finally routines in which the eyes work together in binocular vision. The purpose of these routines is to strengthen through practice the brain's ability to instruct the convergence system without the help of the focus mechanism. The typical course of treatment consists of a weekly visit of forty-five minutes over four to six months, depending on the severity of the problem and the patient's progress.

Our success rate of more than 90 percent is by clinical measure. That is the percentage of patients whose tests after therapy show that they have overcome this problem. What concerns patients, of course, is not so much our tests as how they feel and how they now can perform in their daily lives. By the measure of satisfaction on the part of patients—patients who tell us their problems have been resolved to their satisfaction, that they have gotten what they came to us for —our rate of success is even higher.

Visual perception provides a second set of problems for older people. Their ability to process visual information and act efficiently on it diminishes over the years. We see the evidence in the older driver's slowness in responding to what he sees and in a general awkwardness that testifies to poorer coordination between the eyes and the body.

Some decline in visual perception is inevitable in most people as they reach their later years. But older people who restrict their activities make the problem far worse than it need be. Our perceptual system needs constant practice to keep it accurately tuned. We get that practice in the simplest of everyday actions. Every time we reach for an object, every step we take, we are exercising our perception and our visual-motor coordination. The older person who gives up on a normally active way of life, who allows himself to be put on the shelf, is depriving his perceptual system of exercise, and when it is not exercised it will rust away far faster than it otherwise would.

Again, that decline can be reversed by vision therapy. Here we administer sets of activities designed to rebuild such visual-motor skills as eye-hand and eye-foot coordination. (We should note here with gratitude the work of our colleague Morton Davis, who showed that it was possible to help older people regain their visual-motor skills.)

Success in this field is a relative matter. Therapy is unlikely to restore the responses the patient enjoyed when he was twenty-five. However, the older person's way of life does not require those youthful responses. A degree of improvement is what the older person needs. If that improvement is measured by the ultimate satisfaction of our patients, the rate of success runs around 90 percent. The overwhelming majority of our patients report after therapy that their perceptual skills have improved in the ways that matter to them in their daily lives. This patient can thread a needle—again. Another can drive safely—again. Still another can drive a nail without hitting a finger. For many, it means less risk of the fall that could put them in a hospital for many months. For some it means they feel they can continue to live independently. In their various ways patients find themselves resuming activities they had forsaken. Not only does this enrich the quality of their lives, but by giving the perceptual system ample practice it slows the inevitable decline caused by time. It adds active years to their life-span.

There is an enormous unmet need among our growing population of older people. Just how great that need is may be suggested by the response to an article published in the September 1988 *Bulletin of the American Association of Retired Persons*. The message of the article was that older people were not seeking the visual help they needed. The article ended with a note "for more information" which gave the telephone number of the National Center for Vision and Aging. The switchboard was swamped as soon as the article appeared. A month later they were still averaging a hundred calls a day from older people wanting to know where to go for help. And that was only one of the two telephone numbers listed.

· · ·

Great numbers of older people suffer from very severe visual handicaps that are described as "low vision." The term refers to a visual
impairment so severe that it cannot be corrected by an ordinary lens.

Such people are truly crippled. Their handicaps are far more de-
bilitating than those we described earlier in this chapter. Many qualify as legally blind. The inability to read is their most common
complaint. Some have given up trying; some can read nothing smaller
than a tabloid headline. Some cannot recognize a friend across the
room. They cannot navigate accurately in their homes, and they are
afraid to go out for fear of a fall or a collision. The space in which
they can function is small. Their lives are tragically restricted.

It need not be. Most victims of low vision—from two-thirds to
three-quarters—can in fact be helped. Devices exist with which such
a patient can make the most of what vision remains to him. In recent
years these devices have been made more versatile and effective, and
so the aid available to low-vision sufferers is that much greater than it
was not long ago.

With help, the low-vision patient can come a long way, but, unlike
the person with convergence insufficiency, he cannot come all the
way back to normal vision. Today at least, some degree of loss has to
be accepted as permanent. Yet within those limits people can make
improvements in their vision that will dramatically change the quality
of their lives. One woman, for example, is now reading at a rate of 25
words per minute. To a normal reader, that will seem intolerably
slow. Not to her: she had gone a dozen years in which she could read
nothing at all. For a person who was essentially blind, 25 words a
minute is a godsend. Some people with acuity of 20/400 with glasses
(20/200 with glasses in your better eye makes you legally blind) have
been restored to 20/70 or better: in some states, 20/70 is good enough
to qualify for a driver's license. Such people are still handicapped,
but their visual grasp of their world is far better than it was.

Low vision takes two general forms. One is lost acuity—the person's sight is so poor that it is beyond correction by a normal lens.
The second is loss of visual field (see illustration on page 126). This
can be a loss of central or peripheral vision, or one side of the visual
field, and can happen to one or both eyes. In contrast to poor acuity,

(a)

(b)

LOST VISUAL FIELD

This series of photos illustrates the different kinds of loss of visual field. In the loss of central field (b) the person sees normally in periphery but the central field is blurred or blank. Conversely, peripheral field may be lost (c) while central vision remains intact, or one side may be lost (d).

Reproduced by permission from Harold S. Stein, and Bernard J. Slatt and Raymond M. Stein: *The Ophthalmic Assistant,* 5th ed. (St. Louis: C. V. Mosby, 1988).

(c)

(d)

in which everything looks blurred or distorted, vision in such cases is completely blank in some areas, but the same as before in the rest. Loss of visual field is usually the result of disease. Some people suffer a stroke so minor that its only evidence is the loss of part of their visual field. Degeneration of the macula, which is located in the middle of the retina, can cause the loss of central vision. Among the consequences are that a person cannot read, watch television, or recognize faces.

The successful use of a low-vision device requires a considerable commitment on the part of both the patient and the practitioner who supplies it to him. It's not like getting a new prescription for your glasses. The patient may have to accept the idea of wearing an odd-looking device over his eyes. Most important, he has to learn to use the device, and that can take quite a bit of practice and adjustment. This may be particularly true of someone who has not been able to read for a number of years. The device may require new reading habits such as holding the text at an unfamiliar distance from the eyes. In some cases the patient will have to relearn the art of reading, which can take him many months. Some people start with 18-point type—that's THIS SIZE—and with luck work their way gradually down to normal-size letters. Some find it hard at first to walk around or pick up familiar objects while using the device; other patients may need far less training. But no one is going to be able to take full advantage of a low-vision device without some help in learning how to function with it.

The eye doctor must also make a greater than normal commitment. Not only must he provide training with the device, but his examination of the patient should be unusually thorough. Under normal circumstances an eye doctor may spend twenty to thirty minutes examining a patient's eyes and prescribing lenses. But choosing the right low-vision device means, after the patient's eyes have been examined and his vision tested, learning enough about the patient's routines to understand just how his visual handicap affects his daily life. This will usually take three to four hours spread over two visits. (To find a low-vision specialist, ask your eye doctor for a referral or call Binocular Vision Associates at 1-800-245-2773.)

Failure to meet these requirements is responsible for a large number of unused devices. The person who obtains a device he hasn't learned how to use is almost certain to be frustrated in his attempts to work with it. Very soon the device will go in his top dresser drawer, there to stay. The patient, and too often the eye doctor, will reach the obvious but wrong conclusion: "Nothing can be done." Not that way, it's true.

The most common low-vision device is simply glasses with extra-strength lenses. The next most common is magnifiers that may be hand-held or mounted on a stand. Microscopic and telescopic lenses are highly sophisticated devices. The microscopic device is a two-lens system mounted on regular prescription glasses. It dramatically improves the patient's ability to read by magnifying the print so that it can be seen by the healthy part of the eye. The telescopic lens is a miniaturized telescope, also mounted on regular prescription glasses. It has a variable focus that can be adjusted for tasks at both close and distant ranges, such as, for example, reading, watching television, seeing a chalkboard, recognizing faces. A prism lens can compensate to some extent for loss of visual field by pulling the blocked area into the area where vision remains. If, for example, the right field is lost, the prism will pull into the person's intact central vision what he would normally see to the right. All the devices, not just the aids to reading, require a period of learning and adjustment.

It should be noted that these low-vision devices are useful only in cases where both eyes are severely afflicted. This is because the one good eye, if there is one, will substitute for the afflicted eye and render the device superfluous. Suppose, for example, that a person has 20/1000 sight (virtual blindness) in one eye, and 20/20 in the other. Obviously that person is seeing with the one good eye. A telescopic lens could restore the poorer eye to 20/200, but the patient would continue to rely on the other, better eye without making use of the eye with the new lens. In cases of loss of visual field, the prism lens is useful only when both eyes have suffered a similar loss.

There are also other, nonoptical ways in which the poorly sighted patient's life can be made easier. Many of these have to do with household arrangements. Older people need stronger lighting. Adding vivid color contrast is a great help; a white plate is much more visible on a dark- than a light-colored table. Dials are available that can be read by touch rather than by sight. A growing number of books is published every year in large-type editions. There are even oversized playing cards for those who cannot read anything but a headline.

Vision therapy can also help the low-vision patient. His loss of sight is likely to leave his visual skills in poor shape. A treatment program aimed at repairing those skills can enable him to take full advantage of his low-vision device.

Not all victims of low vision are old. Although most such people are over sixty, a substantial number of children suffer from these kinds of visual defects. These are the people who as a rule have the most to gain from vision therapy. This is because their low vision dates from their very early years. The older patient who loses vision later in life was able, in his childhood, to develop his visual skills in normal fashion. His skills may now be rusty, but at least he has had them. But the visual defects of most young people date from birth or a disease in infancy. They have never experienced the normal childhood growth of vision. They are doubly handicapped—by low vision and by lack of visual skills. Therapy that gives such patients the visual skills they have never had can greatly increase the use they can make of a low-vision device. Such a case was Daniel S.:

•

When DANIEL S. was an infant, doctors told his parents that his optic nerve had been "burned out," and that there was virtually no hope he would ever see well enough to read. The parents, however, refused to accept that verdict. Although Daniel was badly handicapped, he managed to get through school. He learned to read with large-type books, but he never read well and avoided reading whenever possible. Anything involving the use of his eyes was very difficult for him.

In his late teens, Daniel was referred to a low-vision clinic. There he was fitted with a magnifying device that enabled him to see better for close work. The clinic referred him to us for vision therapy to accompany his new device.

We found, not surprisingly, that Daniel was seriously deficient in visual skills. In such perceptual skills as eye-hand coordination, visual memory, and the ability to distinguish figure from ground, he performed at the level of a six-year-old. We could do nothing about his binocular skills because he lacked the physical base on which to build. Accordingly, we concentrated on his perceptual skills.

After a year and a half of therapy Daniel's vision was greatly improved. From the clinical point of view, his perceptual skills had risen in that time from the six-year-old level to the eleven-year-old. That is an enormous gain for someone so handicapped in his vision. Daniel was functioning far more effectively. He completed a course in baking school that, his parents believe, he could not have managed before. At this writing he is planning to open his own bakery with his parents' help, thus exhibiting a measure of independence that had seemed impossible a year earlier. With the combination of vision therapy and his low-vision device, Daniel is far better able to handle the printed word. He reads much more easily and has even taken up crossword puzzles. He sees better even without the device, which is for close work. This has given him much more self-assurance in seemingly simple but once-difficult undertakings like walking around town. He rides a bicycle now and even rode a moped on a vacation trip to Bermuda. Daniel S.'s vision will never be completely normal. But therapy plus his low-vision device have enabled this once-dependent young man to lead a self-reliant life.

•

9

SPORTS AND VISION

Back in the days when he was the American League's outstanding hitter, Ted Williams used to say that he could actually see his bat meet the ball. Many people knowledgeable about eyesight and baseball scoffed at his claim. Nobody could see *that* well, they said.

Years later, long after his playing days were over, Williams demonstrated his exceptional vision to a skeptical umpire named Ron Luciano. As Luciano recounted the event in his book *The Umpire Strikes Back*, Williams coated a bat with pine tar and began hitting pitches. At each hit he would tell Luciano what part of the ball the bat had met: "one seam," "a quarter-inch off the seam," etc. Each time Luciano checked the ball to see if it was marked with tar where Williams had said he hit it. Williams called five out of seven right.

Hitting a baseball is the most difficult visual accomplishment in athletics. In the major leagues the speed of a pitched ball ranges between 70 and 100 miles an hour. If the ball is moving at 80 miles an hour, it will take four-tenths of a second to reach home plate. Swinging the bat takes the professional player two-tenths of a second. That leaves just two-tenths of a second in which the batter must decide on the basis of what he sees whether to swing at the pitch.

While it might seem that few of us need the eyes of Ted Williams in our daily lives, the fact is that we live in a society that makes increasing demands on our vision. So some measure of his visual abilities would help us to get a promotion, perhaps save a life or write a book, or do something extraordinary; and, on the basic level, just get across the street without being hit by a truck. Some of us also are amateur athletes, and, as we saw in Chapter 7, driving a car calls on many of the visual skills needed in sports.

With a few exceptions like swimming or wrestling, athletics demands a high degree of dynamic visual skill—the ability to see well while either the athlete or another person or an object, or both or all three, is in motion. This is the kind of vision that is not tested in the usual examination where a seated person looks at a chart that is equally motionless. That is static acuity, and testing it does not reveal how well that person would see if either he or the chart were moving.

Until recently even sports professionals tended to accept such a static examination as telling them all they needed to know about an athlete's eyes. Now owners and coaches in growing numbers are insisting on knowing more about the visual skills their players need. Many teams hire vision specialists as consultants to measure athletes' visual skills and suggest training to improve those skills. These consultants also test the visual skills of prospective players the team is considering. They then will look especially for the skills that are most important for that sport. Their information can be vital, for example, to a professional football team deciding whom to choose in the annual draft.

Some athletes who have undergone vision training credit it with making a major difference in their performance on the field. Billy Smith, goalie of the New York Islanders, is one such. Another is Virginia Wade, who gave her eye specialist credit for her Wimbledon victory over Chris Evert. "He speeded up my reflexes and I gained greater effectiveness on the court," she said.

Most sports demand good visual skills, but the requirements differ from sport to sport and sometimes from position to position within a sport. The skills needed differ according to what is happening. In tennis, for example, both player and ball are in motion; in baseball the batter, until he swings, is standing still while the pitched ball is moving; and in golf the player stands still, also until he swings, while the ball is at rest. If we look at each of the visual skills in turn, we will learn more about vision and also perhaps where these skills fit into our own lives, whether or not we are Sunday athletes.

DYNAMIC VISUAL ACUITY

This is the ability to see while you and perhaps what you are looking at are in motion. Imagine trying to read a standard eye chart while you are bouncing on a trampoline, or to read a book while jogging. Many, perhaps most, people will find they do not see nearly as well then as they do when they are sitting in a chair looking at that same chart. Those who still see well while bouncing have vision that is suited especially to sports involving a moving object: a hockey puck, or a ball in baseball, basketball, tennis, and other racquet sports.

Training can improve dynamic acuity. A shortstop who was performing erratically had excellent static sight—he tested at above-average, 20/15—but poor dynamic acuity. Vision therapy improved his dynamic acuity and his performance on the field. According to Dr. Leon Revien, a sports vision consultant, a group of sandlot baseball players found that their collective batting average improved by seventy-two points after vision training, and they only struck out half as often.

EYE-TRACKING

This is the skill that was so highly developed in Ted Williams. Like Williams, Billie Jean King believes she can track the ball until it meets her racquet, at least sometimes. "I swear that sometimes I see it and sometimes I don't," she told us. "When I do, I see the spin of the ball; that's when I'm on top of my game." The player who can follow the ball closer to the point of contact is likelier to hit it well. The player who loses eye contact with the ball early is likely to look away. Then his eyes will lead his head, body, and hands out of position, and he will wonder why he hit that shot so badly.

Most people find it difficult if not uncomfortable to follow the ball to, or close to, the point of contact. There is good reason for this difficulty, for it goes contrary to our daily practice. In most such situations we make a visual judgment, start our motion, and then look away before the action is completed. Imagine, for example, that you are sitting at the dinner table and decide to take a drink of water. You look to locate the glass, start to reach—and look away before your hand has actually reached the glass. We do that because it works in ordinary situations like reaching for that motionless glass. But it doesn't work when hitting that fast-moving little ball, and that is when we have to learn to do it differently. This is a skill that can readily be improved with vision therapy.

Although not many people find it necessary to follow a small round object moving at 100 miles an hour with their eyes, we all need the ability to perform visual tracking—as, for example, in moving our eyes to read this page. For an athlete, how he tracks the ball is important. One can follow something visually by moving the eyes alone or by also moving the head. Whenever possible—and this applies to reading as well as to sports—it is better not to move the head because that extra motion tends to throw off the body's balancing system and to disturb visual concentration. "Keep your eye on the ball" is of course the piece of advice most often repeated, and to it we might add: "Keep your head still." If you have any doubts, watch a batter in the box or a tennis player preparing to return serve or a golfer addressing the ball—but make sure you watch an excellent player and watch the head.

DEPTH PERCEPTION AND EYE-TEAMING

We perceive depth when the slightly different two-dimensional images separately received by the two eyes are fused by the brain into a single three-dimensional picture. One eye alone cannot perceive depth. We can of course figure out depth from a single image on the basis of what we know: my hand is closer than the horizon, that apple is round. But those are conclusions reached on the basis of knowledge, not vision—only in the fused image of the two eyes does depth appear in the picture itself.

Nothing is more characteristic of the athletic eye than good depth perception. One study found that varsity athletes had better depth perception than intramural players, while the intramurals did better than those who played no sports. Another study found that better tennis players had better depth perception than less skilled players.

Our hunter ancestors needed depth perception to locate game and avoid enemies, but there is relatively little call for that skill in the close work that is characteristic of modern times. Reading, working at a desk, staring at a computer screen, even watching television: these are all essentially two-dimensional activities. Most sports, by contrast, provide a lot of visual practice in depth perception.

Baseball, basketball, golf, and tennis and the other racquet games are sports in which the ability to judge depth is especially important. A golfer calculating the distance of an approach shot, a basketball player at the foul line, an outfielder preparing to catch a fly ball, a tennis player going to the baseline to retrieve a lob: all are relying on their ability to perceive depth to tell them where the ball is or where it will be. Billie Jean King once wrote that in judging the potential of young tennis players, she considered depth perception more important than eye-hand coordination or speed on the court. King's own style of play, going to the net at every opportunity, is particularly demanding of depth perception and spatial awareness.

In these sports even a small deficit in depth perception can show up in performance. Under the basket Wilt Chamberlain was one of the greatest players of all time, but at the foul line, where depth perception is crucial, his average was chronically poor. He almost invariably overshot the basket, probably because his depth perception was telling him it was a bit farther away than it really was. Chamberlain tried standing behind the foul line, but even that didn't work. His eyes adjusted to the added distance and he continued to overshoot. Tennis players who, unlike King, prefer to stay on the baseline may do so because they lack her ability to perceive depth.

At the other extreme, archery is a sport that, because the archer sights with a single eye, makes no demand on eye-teaming. When we studied the visual skills of Olympic hopefuls participating in the National Sports Festival in Syracuse, New York, we found a surprising incidence of strabismus, turned eyes, among members of the United States archery team. Several archers had one eye, obviously not the eye they sighted with, that turned either in or out. Probably they chose archery because they were comfortable with its visual demands, though they may never have put that thought into words. Certainly they would have been exceedingly uncomfortable (and less successful) playing baseball.

Since standard eye examinations do not test for this skill, many people with poor depth perception may not be aware of what they are, literally, missing. These are leading indications of inadequate perception of depth:

Misjudging a fly ball
Poor net play in tennis
Inaccurate foul-shooting in basketball
Losing sight of the golf ball on its downward flight
Difficulty judging distance, as, for example, in golf when putting
Slap- or pull-hitting in baseball

●

DAVID H., the editor, went into vision therapy mainly to ease the strain of close work at the desk where he earned his living. He also hoped to improve his tennis game. It was frustrating because no matter how much he played and how many lessons he took, he kept on making the same errors. Instructor after instructor barked at him: "You're too close to the ball!" He didn't really need to be told, for he could feel it in his awkward stance and the way his racquet hit, or mis-hit, the ball. But neither David nor the instructors knew why he was hitting the ball too close.

He found out when he came to have his vision tested. A standard test called the Brock String (see illustration, p. 108) showed that David's sense of space was misinforming him. It was telling him that things, including a tennis ball, were farther away than they really were. The cause lay in his eye-teaming. His eyes had a strong tendency to diverge, so when he tried to bring them together they always joined their images a bit beyond the object he wanted to look at.

In the next four months David H. took intensive vision therapy. By coincidence, he did not play tennis during those months. Then he had a chance to play daily for a month. His first day on the court he noticed that the world of tennis looked somehow different. He seemed to see the court in greater depth, with more sense of three dimensions. It was an agreeable, sensuous feeling, as if his view of that familiar scene had been deepened and enriched. The ball looked bigger and yellower and fuzzier. It seemed to move more slowly, almost to hang in the air like a fruit waiting to be eaten. After a few days, David was playing better than he ever had. He could sustain a rally longer. Now he more often experienced that satisfying this-is-what-it's-all-about feeling when his racquet met the ball in what tennis players call the sweet spot. David knows he will not be invited to play at Wimbledon this year or any other. But, in his sixties, he is playing better and enjoying it more. He curses himself less, gives himself more pats on the back. He hadn't planned on Wimbledon anyway.

•

EYE-HAND COORDINATION

So far we have been describing skills of vision alone. Eye-hand coordination involves our response to visual information. We are using the familiar term for it, but it would be more accurate to call it "eye-body coordination" since much more than the hands is usually at work. Vision, brain, and body are all involved: vision to tell us what is happening out there, brain to decide what to do on the basis of that information, body to carry out the brain's orders.

Eye-hand coordination is one of the first skills we begin to practice as infants and of course we use it in almost everything we do in our daily rounds. Any sport that makes use of a ball calls for a high degree of eye-hand coordination—or, in the case of soccer, eye and foot and sometimes head—and when Ted Williams's bat meets the ball we are seeing the ultimate in the split-second coordination of vision, brain, and body.

An interesting sidelight here concerns size and skill. Almost everyone who follows sports will agree that today's basketball players would overwhelm their counterparts of, say, thirty-five years ago. The same is true of football. Not baseball: in this sport most people think that the best players of the past would probably beat today's best. Imagine that this year's all-stars were matched against this team of players active thirty-five years ago:

1B: Stan Musial
2B: Jackie Robinson
3B: Eddie Matthews
SS: Ernie Banks
OF: Willie Mays, Joe DiMaggio, Ted Williams, Mickey Mantle

C: Roy Campanella
P: Robin Roberts, Warren Spahn, Bob Feller

Most, if not all, baseball watchers would bet on the old-timers to win. Why the difference between baseball and the other two sports? Today's football and basketball players would win by virtue of their greater size and speed; athletes are bigger and faster these days. But in hitting a baseball, what matters is not size but eye-hand coordination, and that hasn't improved over the years. If today's baseball all-stars would lose, it is because they haven't developed their visual skills as well as the old-timers did.

The emphasis in "eye-hand" should be on the eye, for it is vision that leads the body. Too often the hands are blamed for faults that belong elsewhere. People who drop things repeatedly are called "clumsy," with the implication that their hands are responsible. More likely, the fault lies in the person's vision. The hands, after all, are doing only what they are told to do. Their performance can be no better than the instructions they get.

Similarly, athletes are said to have "bad hands" when that is not their problem. Blanton Collier, who coached the Cleveland Browns for eight years, wrote: "We discovered that many pass receivers and kick returners would unconsciously look away from the ball a few inches before it hit their hands. Watch the great punt returners and you will see the head pop down as the ball hits their hands. Many receivers who are said to have poor hands because they muff so many pass receptions, don't have poor hands at all. They simply don't visually follow the ball all the way into their hands." Collier wrote that he was "obsessed with the idea that the proper use of the eyes can improve athletic performance" and that he believed vision specialists should play an important role in advising coaches and players.

"Keep your eyes on the ball" means keep them there until the end, till the ball is caught or hit or kicked. Renaldo "Skeets" Nehemiah, the great hurdler, found this out when he signed up for professional football and had to learn to catch passes. He was dropping a lot of passes at first. Later Nehemiah told a reporter that his coach had informed him he was taking his eye off the ball before he caught it. "He said, 'Look the ball into your hands. Tuck it away.' I started doing that, I caught a few, and I relaxed."

PERIPHERAL VISION

Magic Johnson, star of the Los Angeles Lakers, passes over his shoulder to a teammate—a play made possible by his outstanding peripheral vision.

UPI Photo

An oddity of sports vision is that many good baseball hitters have crossed dominance. The dominant eye is the one that leads the eyes in locating the target. Most of us have our dominant hand and eye on the same side, but a few do not. In batting, crossed dominance is an advantage because when a right-handed batter stands at the plate his left eye is closer to the pitcher and so in a better position to lead his vision and pick up the target a fraction of a second earlier. (The same is true, in reverse, of the left-hander.) If you are wondering which eye is dominant in your own case, here is a simple way to find out. Make a circle with your thumb and forefinger. With both eyes open, center an object in your sight in that circle. Now close each eye in turn. The eye in which that object is still centered in the ring of your fingers is your dominant one.

PERIPHERAL VISION

We see most clearly in the central field of vision, a restricted zone that extends straight out from the center of the retina. In the much larger surrounding field our sight is not so acute. We see differently in the two zones of sight. In the central field we see objects in sharp detail and not necessarily related to each other. In the larger periphery we do not see detail but instead we see movement and the relationships in space among things and people. In his book *The Ultimate Athlete*, George Leonard called this the difference between seeing with "hard eyes" (central) and "soft eyes" (peripheral).

Like depth perception, peripheral vision is a skill that is little needed in the daily close work that occupies so many of us. A student reading, an accountant totaling figures, a dentist drilling: they are all working entirely in the central field of vision. Our hunter ancestors needed peripheral vision more than most of us do in our modern lives.

Athletes do need it. Most sports, with exceptions like bowling, require good peripheral vision. The pitcher on the mound is concentrating on the batter before him, but he also must be aware without turning his head of the runner on first base. Particularly in doubles, a tennis player must keep her eyes on the ball she is about to hit and at the same time be aware of what her opponents and her partner are doing. Barbara Potter said: "When you're dialed into the ball it's a very central object, and yet you have to have peripheral awareness of where your opponent is in the court. I call this a feel. I like to have a feel for the opponent, the ball, and my position in relation to those two. All three are crucial, although at some point you can't focus on all three with the same intensity at once."

In baseball the batter uses soft and hard focus to fix his attention as early as possible on the ball. As he waits for the pitch, he holds in peripheral soft focus the pitcher's "release zone"—the area within which he knows the pitcher will release the ball. He wants to catch the ball in central hard focus at the very instant of its release, giving himself a vital fraction of a second more in which to judge the pitch and respond.

Basketball is the sport in which we see the most superlative examples of peripheral vision. A great player makes things happen because of his ability to take in everything that is going on all over the court. On some plays it seems as if he has eyes in the back of his head. In the case of Bill Bradley, that was proved almost true. Bradley, the New York Knicks star who at this writing is a United States senator, once had his peripheral vision tested at the request of writer John McPhee. In his book *A Sense of Where You Are*, McPhee said he made the request after he had noticed Bradley's ability to pass to a man in the open without looking at him. A Princeton ophthalmologist found that Bradley's peripheral vision exceeded the doctor's definition of the ideal. The most the person with normally good peripheral vision is able to see on a horizontal plane while looking ahead is 180 degrees. Bradley could see across an arc of 195 degrees. On the vertical plane, where the good eye can see 70 degrees, Bradley achieved 75 degrees.

Peripheral vision, like other visual skills, improves with practice and grows rusty with disuse. Young Bill Bradley knew that without being told. He told McPhee that when he was young he used to walk down the street identifying the goods in the store windows he was passing while keeping his eyes straight ahead.

VISUAL REACTION TIME

If eye-hand coordination determines how well we respond to what we see, visual reaction time defines how fast we respond. To an athlete one is as important as the other. Most sports call for both good coordination and quick response. Just as there is no use making the

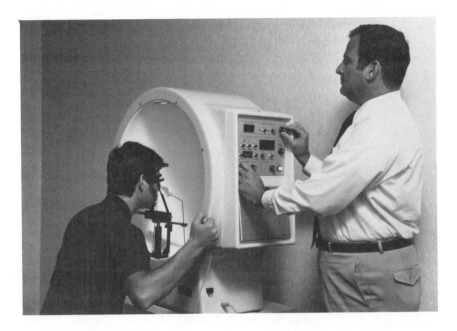

TESTING PERIPHERAL AWARENESS

The patient keeps his eyes fixed on a target at the center of the space ahead of him and registers, with the button in his right hand, when he sees lights flashed to one side or the other. The computer itself records where his eyes are directed and will not register his scores if he looks away from the target. The panel at the right displays his scores.

wrong play in time, there is also no use making the right play if it is too late.

A hockey goalie is an example of a player whose reaction time is crucial. The puck comes sliding across the ice at 100 miles an hour and often the goalie's view is obstructed so that he does not see the puck till it is almost upon him. The smallest fraction of a second in the goalie's reaction time can make the difference between blocking the puck and letting it through. Similarly, the quarterback's speed in responding when he sees an open receiver will determine whether he gets the pass off or is sacked with the ball still in his hands.

Not all sports require fast visual response. The skill is unimportant in sports like golf and billiards where time is not an immediate factor. On the other hand, driving a car and speed-reading are two very different nonathletic activities in which fast visual response is essential.

In tennis the importance of visual response varies with the style of play. A player who goes to the net has less than half as much time as a baseliner to respond when his opponent hits the ball. Bill Drake, Tim Mayotte's coach, has said: "You pick up the ball as soon as the reflexes in your eyes channel it to the brain and start you moving your feet. Obviously, there is variation in individual skills in this area, but I would think that if athletes could be trained to pick up the ball sooner, even if it is a fraction of a second, this would be a magnificent factor toward winning matches."

In fact, athletes, and anyone else, can be trained to pick up the ball sooner. If, for example, you flash a number on a wall in front of seven athletes for one one-hundredth of a second, only two are likely to identify it. The other five will miss it. But give those five training on the tachistoscope, the instrument that flashes the numbers on the wall, and before long most if not all of them will see what the first two saw. That increased speed will carry over into sports or reading or any other activity.

VISUALIZATION

This most abstract of visual skills takes place entirely in the mind. It is the ability to see in your mind's eye the particular moves you will make in a given situation. You are in fact practicing, for experiments have shown that when you visualize doing something, the muscles involved in that activity respond by contracting. Your body is rehearsing along with your mind.

The value of visualization was demonstrated in a well-known study conducted by Alan Richardson with student basketball players. Richardson divided them into three groups. One group was told to practice shooting fouls twenty minutes daily for twenty days. The second group practiced only twice, on the first and twentieth days. The third group, like the second, practiced only twice on the court, but they also spent twenty minutes a day practicing in their heads. In their mind's eye they saw the arc of the ball from when it left their hands till it went through the basket. If it missed, they adjusted their imaginary position and threw till they got it right. The results were surprising. The first group, those who practiced every day, improved by 24 percent. The second group did not improve at all. And the third group, those who practiced mainly by visualizing, improved by 23 percent, almost as much as those who practiced daily on the court.

In golf every shot requires visualizing. Before he putted, Ben Hogan would visualize the ball dropping into the cup. Jack Nicklaus describes what he does: "I go to the movies in my head. . . . First I see the ball where I want it to finish. . . . Next I see the ball going there. . . . Finally I see myself making the kind of swing that will turn the first two images into reality."

On the value of visualization in tennis, Barbara Potter says: "When I'm visualizing well, I tend to hit the ball better than when I have no image of what I want to do on the next point. On return of serve, I like to visualize placement, as well as the desired spin, whether I hit under the ball or over the ball."

Visualization is essential in a fast-moving sport like football. As he waits for a play to start, a good player will visualize in detail what he would do in one or another situation. The point is that once play starts he will not have time to decide how to execute an action. His mind and body must be ready, and so he rehearses them. The fraction of a second he saves may make the difference. Visualization also serves the purpose of estimating what opposing players will do. By seeing himself in the other person's bodily stance, the player can tell what his opponent can and cannot do from that position, and he can prepare accordingly. If, for example, his visual image tells him the other player cannot easily go to his left, he will prepare for his opponent's going to his right.

Vince Papale, once a great wide receiver for the Philadelphia Eagles, recalls his playing days: "I visualize my pass patterns, how I'm going to get open and make a catch. I can sit here and see myself making the hook pattern, exactly how I'm going to break free. Visualization was also a key for me when I first made the Eagles. They wanted me to run a forty-yard dash. The night before I went onto the starting line, I actually saw myself as a graceful, smooth, fluid animal; not an athlete, not Vince Papale, but like an animal. I just tried to picture being very smooth, very relaxed, and graceful. I went out and I ran a four-five, which was unbelievable for a thirty-year-old rookie with no professional or college football experience."

All this is not to say that wishing will make it so. You may imagine yourself stepping up to the service line, racquet back, tossing the ball, and aceing your opponent—Jimmy Connors! That is obviously not going to happen, nor will that delightful fantasy even improve your game unless you know what you are doing. That is the difference between visualization and fantasy. Visualization is rehearsing, and, just as an actor cannot rehearse lines he does not know, a player cannot rehearse moves he has not learned. The muscles do not know what to practice. Of course, even if you do it right you still won't ace Jimmy Connors—but you can improve your serve. You might ace your spouse.

ACCOMMODATION

Accommodation is the ability to change focus from one point to another. When it is discussed in sports, it is always accompanied by a closely related skill, convergence, which is the eyes' ability to align precisely together.

Golf and tennis are two sports that require good accommodation and convergence. In golf, shifting the focus from the pin on the green to the ball in front of you requires instant accommodation. No sport asks more of the accommodative system than billiards. A good pool player focuses and refocuses in three directions: first to the pocket where he wants the ball to go, then to the spot on the cushion where he wants the ball to hit and ricochet, and finally to the tip of his cue. His sight must clear immediately each time he refocuses.

Focusing skills decline with age. The forty-year-old tennis player who says "I don't know what's wrong but my timing is way off" may be suffering from deteriorating ability to accommodate. So may the golfer whose sight does not clear promptly when he shifts focus from the green to the ball. Middle-aged athletes should have their accommodation skills checked periodically. Sometimes convex lenses, usually prescribed for farsightedness, can correct the problem.

VISUAL CONCENTRATION

Concentration follows visualization. It means the ability to focus visual attention during the play itself after we have rehearsed in the mind's eye.

"Concentration in any sport is probably 90 percent visually related," said Mike Schmidt, two-time Most Valuable Player with the Philadelphia Phillies. "Eyesight and preparation are the two most important factors in staying concentrated out on the ball field. By preparation, I mean the pre-game activity I follow to get myself ready for an act out on the field. For example, I may have to mentally prepare myself for catching ground balls on a dirt field instead of on Astroturf. So when my pitcher is warming up, I prepare myself mentally to react to a ball hit my way. When the ball is hit, however, I have to watch it go into my glove. I have to visually react to it; I have to be visually very concentrated."

Concentration is both a state of mind and a visual skill. To illustrate, here is Dave LaPoint of the St. Louis Cardinals describing his pitching against the Milwaukee Braves in the 1982 World Series: "I got in my bubble of concentration right away. Sometimes you'll hear the crowd, or pick out somebody in the stands. All I saw today was [catcher] Darrel Porter's finger and Darrel Porter's glove. You have to be like that or you won't be around very long."

Centering on a small target helps one to concentrate. Blanton Collier, former coach of the Cleveland Browns, was the first to advocate centering in football. He told his quarterbacks to aim not at the pass receiver but at some part of his anatomy: chest, shoulder, hip. One of his quarterbacks, Frank Ryan, said: "This target idea is the single most important thing that's ever been told to me but the toughest thing I've ever tried to do. But if you do it, it will improve your efficiency by about ten to fifteen percent." On the other end of the throw, Vince Papale has said that concentrating on the tip instead of the entire football seemed to slow the ball down and increase his chance of catching it.

Bill Bradley applied the same principle to basketball. After setting a record at Princeton by sinking twenty-one foul shots in a row, Bradley explained that he concentrated not on the basket but on one of the small steel eyelets welded under the rim of the basket.

The idea of concentrating visual attention on a small target is not new. The *Mahabharata*, the Hindu epic, tells the story of Drona, the master archer, testing the students he has taught. The target for their test is a bird made of straw and cloth hung high in a tree. Drona calls each student in turn. While the first student is taking aim, Drona asks him: "What do you see?" "The tree and the bird, the bow and the arrow, and my arm and you." Drona dismisses him. The same happens to the following students. Then the master archer summons Arjuna, the hero of the epic, and puts the same question: "What do you see?" "A bird." "Describe him to me." "I cannot; I see only his neck." "Send that arrow!"

Arjuna's arrow cut the head from the target. He had learned his lesson in visual concentration.

●

VISION AND THE YOUNG ATHLETE

As we saw in earlier chapters, human vision is not fully developed until the age of ten or eleven and sometimes later. So a game that is visually very demanding, like baseball, will be particularly hard on the youngster whose vision has not completely developed, as is in fact the case with many Little League players. The visual skills needed in sports are also needed, though in different degree, in the classroom. In Chapter 4 we listed signs of visual disorders that teachers and parents should watch for. In sports, coaches—and again, parents—should be on the watch for other indications that may signal a disorder in vision. Here are the most common signs, arranged according to the visual skills to which they refer:

EYE-TEAMING
Difficulty catching a fly ball
Excessive eye-rubbing or blinking
Constantly misjudging the distance to the basket
Inability to serve or hit an overhead shot in tennis
Frequently running into teammates or opposing players

ACCOMMODATION
Seems unduly tired, though in good physical condition
Reports blurred vision after practice in school, but not on weekends
Reports blurred vision as the school day progresses
Has trouble adjusting visually from near to far, or far to near

EYE MOVEMENTS

Jerky or erratic eye movements
Frequent movement of head to follow the ball
Inability to hit a baseball
Difficulty tracking a tennis ball
Inability to head a soccer ball accurately
Short attention span

EYE-HAND COORDINATION

Poor contact in hitting: player may hit a few home runs but strikes out often
Tennis player has good form but makes poor contact with ball
Difficulty learning Ping-Pong, badminton, volleyball
Inability to bounce a kickball or basketball more than three times consecutively
Trouble playing a simple game of catch: drops ball frequently

10

CAN MYOPIA BE CURED?

Until very recently, the answer to the question Can myopia be cured? was an emphatic no. Opinions differed on its cause, but almost everyone in the field of eye care agreed that once a person had become nearsighted nothing could be done beyond fitting him with corrective lenses.

Now, however, a treatment program that includes a therapeutic instrument based on the principle of biofeedback has made it possible to stop and reverse the development of myopia in thousands of people of different ages and with varying degrees of nearsightedness. The Accommotrac, as the device is called, holds out hope to almost all kinds of myopes. Among them, three very large groups are likely to find particularly great benefits: young people who are just becoming nearsighted, adults whose myopia is getting worse, and middle-aged people who are facing the need for bifocals.

This is news of the utmost importance, for nearsightedness is by far the most common of visual defects. About one-quarter of Americans are myopic, and among adults who spend their days doing close work with their eyes the proportion rises to more than half. What's more, as we saw earlier, these percentages are rising so rapidly in modern societies that it is no exaggeration to say we are experiencing an epidemic of nearsightedness.

Given its prevalence, it comes as no surprise that an enormous amount of research has been devoted to myopia. Thousands of studies have been published on various aspects of the subject. Underlying this work have been two basic questions: Is myopia inherited or acquired? Can anything be done about it?

The optics of myopia have been understood for a long time. Light entering the eye is bent inward toward the retina first by the cornea and second by the lens, which fine-tunes the work of the cornea. (See illustration on p. 153.) The action of the cornea is fixed, while the lens, by changing its shape, adjusts the focus of the picture so that in the normal eye it falls clearly on the retina. In the myopic eye, the focus falls short of the retina; as a result, the image received of distant objects is blurred. A corrective lens compensates for the insufficient action of the lens and makes the image fall clearly on the retina.

Why myopia happens is not so certain. A small number of people, only about 1 percent, are born myopic. In these cases the eye is abnormally large from front to back, with the result that the lens is too far from the retina and so the focus falls short of its destination.

The overwhelming majority of nearsighted people become so during the first twenty years of life. Most myopes get progressively more nearsighted until their late teens or early twenties, when the condition levels off. Nearsightedness comes very fast to a great many people. By age ten, one person in ten is nearsighted. By age fourteen the number doubles to 20 percent, and by eighteen it doubles once more, to 40 percent. In the next few years it rises to 50 percent.

Those are of course the years of schooling—and a great deal of reading. What happens to those who become nearsighted then has to do with the ciliary, the ring-shaped muscle behind the iris that controls the lens and therefore the focus. When our eyes are at rest or focused on a distant target, the ciliary is relaxed, also at rest—another reminder that our eyes were designed to look at the horizon rather than the telephone book. To focus on a near target, the ciliary contracts and this pushes the lens into a more convex shape.

In some people, when the ciliary is asked to remain tense for long stretches of time, as in prolonged reading, the little muscle goes into a spasm. It finds it increasingly difficult to relax as it must to alter the shape of the lens and focus at distance. The spasm of the ciliary increases the pressure of the liquid that keeps the eyeball in shape. The added pressure pushes the front of the eye forward, increasing the distance from lens to retina, so that when the lens focuses on a distant target the focus falls short and the image on the retina is blurred.

In recent years scientific evidence has challenged the long-standing

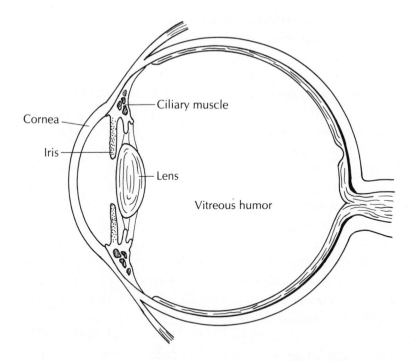

THE CILIARY MUSCLE AND THE LENS

belief that myopia is inherited. Francis Young, in a landmark series
of experiments in the 1960s, showed that monkeys become nearsighted when the range of their sight is restricted to less than 20
inches. Young's findings were confirmed in the 1970s by Torsten
Weisel and Elio Raviola, who sutured together the eyelids of monkeys. Again, the monkeys became nearsighted.

Does the great amount of close work we do in school cause the
myopia that comes in those years? The evidence is compelling that
the two go hand in hand. The connection was noticed as long ago as
1813. In that year an English ophthalmologist, James Ware, reported
that nearsightedness was found among one-quarter of Oxford students applying for army commissions but was far less frequent among
ten thousand unschooled farmers and fishermen in the enlisted ranks.
Earlier we mentioned two studies, of Eskimos and Japanese, that
found the same connection, and many other researchers have reported
similar results.

A very large study was made recently by two Israeli physicians, who compared myopia with years in school among 157,748 youths aged seventeen to nineteen who had been screened for military service. At every level, the two doctors wrote in 1987, more schooling meant more nearsightedness. Among those who had completed eight or fewer years of school, 7.5 percent were myopic. The rate of nearsightedness rose steadily with years in school to 19.7 percent among those with twelve or more years of education.

The Israeli researchers also found what appeared to be a correlation between nearsightedness and intelligence. On average, myopes scored higher on intelligence tests than normal or farsighted people. The Israelis were not the first to notice this; other researchers from California to Great Britain to New Zealand have reported similar results. But nearsighted people should not jump to the conclusion that, as they may have suspected all along, they are smarter than the rest of us. More likely, and the studies suggest this, something else is going on. People who do well in school tend to stay there longer and so to read more because that's where they are successful. They also do well on tests, including intelligence tests. More years in school spell both more nearsightedness and better test scores—hence the apparent connection between the two.

"Fight or flight," in the words of our colleague Richard Kavner, are two of the schoolchild's possible responses when his hunter's eyes are asked to do more close work than they can handle. The fight response is the one we have described: these children force the ciliary to do the required work and, in time, half of them become nearsighted. Those who choose flight simply give up the struggle. They refuse to force their eyes to read. They avoid work that involves reading, they become known as "underachievers," they join the ranks of those we call "learning-disabled."

Observing the link between visually demanding close work and myopia did not of itself supply a cure. Once the child was myopic, eye doctors could do no more than go on prescribing the lenses that restored him to a normal 20/20. However, there are ways to do this that are far better for the child than those practiced by the majority of eye doctors. We developmental optometrists often prescribe dual-focus lenses for myopic schoolchildren to mitigate the impact of reading stress. The usual single-lens glasses provide the needed correction for seeing at distance, but that same lens can cause unnecessary stress when used for close work. In dual-focus glasses, the myopia correction is for distance only, with a different stress-reducing prescription in the lower part for close work. This use of bifocals can slow the advance of myopia but obviously cannot reverse the process.

Another way of delaying the onset of myopia has to do with the time at which children are asked to read and is based on an experiment conducted in the public schools of Cheshire, Connecticut, by John W. Streff, a developmental optometrist. Two changes were made in the lives of children in the first five grades. The first was that they were grouped according to their "behavioral age." This had the effect of delaying the time at which children with immature visual systems were started on reading. The second change was that teachers were asked to add to the day a half-hour of problem-solving games intended to develop visual-motor skills. When Streff tested the children in sixth grade, he found that the level of myopia was substantially less than in the three control groups he also tested. We believe that applying the lessons of Streff's work would delay the onset of myopia and perhaps reduce its severity. But this approach by itself cannot cure myopia, any more than can stress-reducing lenses.

(A school of thought that did believe myopia could be cured was based on the theories of the American ophthalmologist William Bates. In his 1918 book *Better Eyesight Without Glasses*, Bates prescribed a series of visual training exercises. The Bates method was popularized by Aldous Huxley in his bestselling book *The Art of Seeing*. The method enjoyed a vogue in the 1940s, but most people found the training too long and tedious and the results too uncertain to stay with it. Its validity was never scientifically established.)

Understanding the role of the ciliary muscle and its spasm provided the necessary clue to Dr. Joseph Trachtman, a young optometrist from Brooklyn Heights. Trachtman thought the answer could be found in the principle of biofeedback. Biofeedback is a method of informing a person about those involuntary operations of his body which he is not aware of and does not consciously control, the heartbeat being a familiar example and the ciliary being another. It has been successfully used in treating high blood pressure, migraine headaches, and digestive disorders. Trachtman believed that it should be possible to harness biofeedback to relieve the stress in the ciliary, which is controlled by the autonomic, or involuntary, nervous system. He set out to invent an instrument that could do it. It took him seven years to make and test that instrument.

The result of Trachtman's work is the device he calls the Accommotrac. The patient gazes, one eye at a time, into an eyepiece where he sees only white light. There is nothing on which his eye can focus and so it tends to relax. The instrument sends a harmless beam of infrared light into his eye aimed at the lens. The reflection of this light reports the changing shape of the lens and therefore the relaxed or tense state of the ciliary muscle. It reports change at the rate of 40 times a second. Then—and this is the key to the Accommotrac—the machine translates that information into sound the patient can hear. The instrument can provide seven kinds of sound (based, by the way, on video games); it can translate ciliary change into sound that goes higher or lower or faster or slower. The patient chooses the type of sound and change that best suits him. The instrument greatly amplifies what is happening to the muscle so that even a slight change will be audible to the patient. At the same time that it is reporting to the patient in sound, the instrument translates the same information into a graph and into numbers, so that the therapist, who sits opposite the patient, gets the news in two forms in addition to the sound.

The therapist asks the patient to try to make the sound go higher (or whatever represents the relaxing of the ciliary). The patient experiments with various ways to relax until he finds one that works—and for the first time in his life he learns from the change in sound that it *is* working. This immediate feedback enables the patient to connect the relaxing of his ciliary to whatever else he was doing or experiencing at the time. His goal is to find a voluntary action—imagining a sound or a landscape, or relaxing a voluntary muscle—that will trigger the involuntary response of the ciliary. After a session with the instrument, the therapist will test the patient's sight on an eye chart. Usually this will show an improvement even on the first visit. This early improvement is transitory but is nonetheless important, for it provides the patient with the first evidence of the basic principle of all vision therapy: that he can make his vision better by his own efforts.

In repeated visits the patient practices his ability to translate the changing sound into a relaxed ciliary muscle. At home he practices doing it without the sound, with an eye chart on which he can see the improvement in his sight. He may imagine the sound or else re-create a sensation he felt when he was sitting at the Accommotrac. Eventually, when the treatment is successful, he becomes able to relax his ciliary at will. Thus he eliminates the spasm that caused the buildup in pressure in his eyeball, and with that he has (except in the small minority of congenital cases) eliminated the cause of his myopia.

The myopia control program works, and the Accommotrac is a useful adjunct to it. The theory of biofeedback has proved itself in practice. By now several thousand patients have been successfully treated. Some of these are patients of Trachtman himself, who began using the Accommotrac in his practice in 1981, but an increasing proportion are patients of other eye doctors. The authors began using the Accommotrac in August 1987.

Seven New Jersey eye doctors reported in 1985 the results of their study of sixteen patients who used the Accommotrac. The patients were aged nine to thirty-seven, and their myopia ranged from mild (20/30) to severe (20/400). All sixteen patients were less nearsighted after treatment. The 20/30 patient regained normal sight of 20/20, while at the other extreme, the 20/400 patient got down to 20/100; those in between improved their sight without reaching 20/20. This accords with Trachtman's own report on eighty-four patients. These patients started with sight ranging from 20/20 to 20/1000, with a median of 20/200. After an average of eight sessions with the Accommotrac, these patients' sight ranged from 20/15 to 20/200, with a median of 20/30—a very large improvement. Our own experience with the instrument confirms these findings. We believe that biofeedback training is an important addition to a treatment program that typically will also include vision therapy to correct binocular disorders, nutritional advice, and counseling on changes in behavior to reduce the visual stress that causes myopia.

The picture that emerges from the experience to date with the myopia control program is that the great majority of nearsighted people can expect substantial improvement and that where they will arrive can be predicted from where they began. The very myopic patient (20/200 or more) can expect a considerably reduced prescription and more comfortable vision without, however, getting all the way back to normal. For those in the area of 20/100, this can make the difference between full- and part-time use of glasses. Most important, but only if he also takes simple measures to lessen the stress of intensive close work, the person with deteriorating sight can expect his myopia to stop getting worse. Someone who is at 20/80 or less stands a very good chance of returning to normal and throwing away his glasses. An example in this category is Rosalie K.

•

ROSALIE K., who is in her forties, had been wearing contact lenses for more than twenty years. She was only moderately nearsighted (20/50), but she wore the contacts for twelve or thirteen hours a day. She worked at a high-pressure job as secretary to a corporate chief executive. She started on the program of vision therapy and biofeedback intending to quit if it did not produce quick results. After her first session, she looked at the eye chart. It was blurred. She thought about what happened when she was on the Accommotrac, and the next-to-last line cleared momentarily. "It seemed incredible," she recalled. She decided to continue.

After four months of two sessions a week, Rosalie's sight had returned to normal. In fact it was 20/16, better than normal. She had given up wearing her contacts along the way and now did not miss them. After twenty years this was a dramatic change in her life. She noticed that for the first time she could recognize people coming down the long hall outside her office. At an eye examination she was asked to look again at a picture of a country scene with what in previous examinations she had seen as just a red car; this time she recognized it as a Porsche. "I laughed to myself," she recalled. "All of a sudden that car had an identity!" Her sport is sailing. Now she scans the horizon for buoys without her contact lenses, something she never thought she'd be able to do.

During therapy Rosalie K. started practicing her concentration on street signs when she was driving or just walking around. She still practices. To break the visual intensity of her work, she takes a moment to gaze out the window. If something is unclear she concentrates, blinks, and it becomes clear. She is always pushing to see a little better, although she says she is "amazed I can see as well as I can."

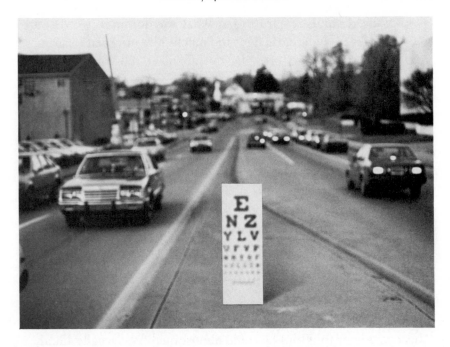

SIGHT AT 20/80 (TOP) AND 20/20

Rosalie K. finds it hard to put what she does into words. "I work my eyes. I glare, then it's too much; I let up, then it clears. By now it's second nature, but it's difficult to tell you just what I do."

•

Rosalie K.'s statement that it is difficult to describe what she does that causes the ciliary muscles in her eyes to relax is typical of patients who have used the Accommotrac. Patients report a wide variety of techniques. Some imagine the change in sound that signals success; others visualize clear sight or a scene that suggests relaxation; for others it is a certain physical sensation. But the common thread that runs through many of their accounts is the difficulty of finding words that adequately describe the process.

•

MICHAEL L., a fifty-year-old chiropractor, was so nearsighted his eye doctor told him he could almost qualify as legally blind. His glasses had gotten as thick as bottle bottoms, so he had changed to contact lenses. Even with the lenses, his sight was far from normal; he could not read the first line on the eye chart. He could not read a restaurant menu by candlelight.

He went into therapy hoping only to reduce his very severe myopia. After several months, his sight had improved by one-third and he was still making progress. He was still wearing his contacts, but the prescription was getting progressively weaker.

Michael L. found he was particularly responsive to the changing sound of the Accommotrac: "My eye feels as if it's expanding. It lets loose and the sound goes 'z-z-z' "—here he imitates the high-pitched whine of a mosquito. He does most of his practicing, like Rosalie K., with road signs when he is driving to and from work. He looks at the sign and concentrates; then in his mind he hears the "z-z-z" and the image of the sign clears. He says, "I can almost feel my eye expanding." His sight with lenses is now better than it has been for many years: "I can read that restaurant menu." Michael L.'s brother and daughter, both nearsighted, have followed him into therapy and are doing well.

•

People who need excellent sight in their work have found they can use biofeedback therapy to repair a loss of vision that might seem small to others but is essential to them. The example that comes immediately to mind is an airline pilot, and that is the occupation of one of our patients:

●

FRANK I. is a former Navy pilot in his forties who flies for a commercial airline. He is of course sensitive to any change in his excellent vision. He found that the sight which used to test at 20/15 in the Navy was now falling off by the end of the day to 20/30, though in the mornings it was still 20/20. He noticed also that his change of focus seemed slower—a potentially critical problem in the cockpit, where a pilot must shift his focus rapidly from written instructions 1 foot from his eyes to the instruments 2 feet away. He was constantly rubbing his left eye, and his right eye seemed "lazy."

After three months of myopia control therapy, Frank I.'s sight was back to better than 20/20 in both eyes. His right eye seemed particularly improved. He believes he is focusing faster. He notices this in the cockpit and also at home when he looks up from the book he is reading to the television his family is watching.

●

Young people who are just beoming myopic are a group that is particularly likely to benefit from myopia control therapy. As we have seen, the overwhelming majority of people who become nearsighted do so in their first twenty years. If their sight at distance is checked annually, as is done in most schools, their myopia can be caught while it is both recent and relatively mild—two factors that increase the probability of success. They can quickly be brought back to normal sight, and there is an excellent chance that they may never have to wear the glasses they would otherwise have needed.

●

CHRIS H., seventeen, flunked the eye test for his driver's permit. His eyes tested at 20/80 and 20/60. He had gotten glasses for distance a year earlier but was reluctant to wear them—he preferred to sit at the front in class and at the movies. Now he was facing the prospect of stronger glasses and having to wear them if he wanted to get his permit. So he agreed to myopia control therapy.

Chris found the therapy "pretty unusual. You don't have to do anything; there's no work involved. You just concentrate on the sound." He began to notice in a couple of weeks that he could read more lines on the eye chart right after he had been on the Accommotrac. But his sight would slip back if he did not keep practicing at home.

After five months of therapy both of Chris's eyes tested at 20/20. His sight still tends to blur when he is tired, but when it does he thinks of the sound getting faster and his sight clears. In school he never has trouble seeing the blackboard.

•

ROBERT J., twelve, was considerably more nearsighted than Chris H. Both eyes tested at 20/100, and the left seemed to be getting rapidly worse. He hated the idea of wearing glasses and was worried that his poor sight would hurt him in sports. He had trouble in school with reading comprehension.

After five months of therapy Robert's sight was back to 20/30 in each eye—close enough to normal for him to do without glasses. His mother reported that his reading was much better and that his basketball had also improved. Robert himself said, "I used to have a lot of trouble seeing things far away. Now I am seeing things more clearly." We discontinued his therapy in the belief that he had reached a plateau and was unlikely to go all the way to 20/20.

•

Another major category of potential beneficiaries of biofeedback treatment is myopes who are beginning to need bifocals. This is that time of life, usually between the late thirties and the early forties, when we notice that the printed page no longer is as clear as it used to be. Oliver Wendell Holmes, Sr., called it the "trombone age," because a person moving the page in and out in a vain effort to get the type into focus reminded him of a trombone player moving his slide in and out.

The condition is called "presbyopia"—meaning literally, "old person's eyes." For many people this time offers their first intimation of mortality, and indeed it is a natural part of the aging process; the big postwar baby-boom generation is now reaching this stage. Starting as early as age fourteen, the lens of the eye gradually loses its flexibility. As the lens stiffens, the ciliary muscle is less and less able to make it change shape. In a myope, the ciliary is already unable to focus for distance; now it cannot make the lens focus at near either. Hence the need for two kinds of correction in the same glasses, or two pairs of glasses.

Myopia control therapy with the Accommotrac has been very successful in enabling this kind of patient to put off the need for bifocals. Trachtman finds that the "forty- to fifty-year-old myope" is his most promising patient, in part because this kind of person usually is highly motivated by his desire to avoid bifocals. The use of the instrument is the same for presbyopia as it is for nearsightedness: the patient learns through the changing sound to control the ciliary muscle and thereby gains greater ability to make the lens focus at near as well as at distance.

The treatment is not limited to myopes. It is also effective for a budding presbyope who is not nearsighted. Such a case was Maureen J.

•

MAUREEN J. had never worn glasses. Now, in her early forties, she was beginning to have trouble with her eyes. The type was blurring when she read, especially in the right eye, and she was holding the page further and further away. Sewing was becoming difficult. When she was tired, any kind of close work was hard to sustain. She was getting headaches.

Five months of biofeedback therapy with the Accommotrac restored to Maureen J. the comfortable sight she used to enjoy. She has no trouble with close work of any kind. She reads a lot now, as she did before she began having trouble with her sight. She has fewer headaches. Except when her eyes are very tired, she can clear any blurring by thinking about the changing sound of the Accommotrac.

•

We have not used the biofeedback/Accommotrac method long enough to be certain as to how enduring its benefits will prove to be. Although thousands of people have been successfully treated, Trachtman did not start treating patients until 1981, and we first began using the instrument in 1987. So we will not know until more years have passed if the nearsighted teenager whose sight is restored to normal will stay there indefinitely or whether in later years he will suffer another onslaught of myopia, perhaps requiring further biofeedback treatment. Nor do we know how long the forty-year-old presbyope will be able to stave off the effects of the gradual stiffening of his lenses.

Nonetheless, the early results, at least, are very encouraging about the durability of the treatment. Trachtman has reported his first three patients as maintaining their improved sight after seven years. We do know that a great deal depends on the patient. Age is not a critical factor; eye doctors have successfully used the therapy with patients younger than ten and older than sixty. Some people, however, seem better able than others to make use of the principle of biofeedback; some such patients will even say after the treatment that they can actually feel their eyes relaxing. Those who do intensive close work must learn to mitigate the effects of their way of life if they are to keep what they gain with therapy. This means periodically interrupting their visual concentration—for example, by gazing out the window at a distant target and relaxing their eyes. It also means following the principles of good eye care and nutrition that we describe in Appendix A.

Nor do we yet know all the ways in which biofeedback can be put to use in vision therapy. The Accommotrac is its first practical application; we are certain that others will follow. Some eye doctors have used the instrument in treating farsightedness. Others have used it in conjunction with standard vision therapy in the treatment of a turned eye. Trachtman believes the instrument can be used in treating glaucoma, which, like myopia, involves an increase in the internal pressure of the eyeball.

Biofeedback has provided vision therapy with a powerful new tool. We will be exploring its potential for years to come.

11

FOR A VISUALLY AWARE WORLD

Suppose that the society we live in were visually aware. Suppose, that is, that we were geared to meet the growing demands on people's vision that we have described in the preceding chapters. This is how that society would differ from the present.

Every school system, from grade school through college, will have its vision consultant. This will not be an "eyeball person"—a description that fits most of today's eye doctors—but rather a doctor who understands that the visual requirements of learning go far beyond 20/20. Today only a small minority of schools have such expert advice available to them (though most have dental consultants). The vision consultant will screen children referred to him; if he finds visual problems, he will inform their parents. He will similarly screen the lowest achievers in the class for visual disorders and also those who appear to be performing below their intellectual capacity. He will be a member of the evaluation team that advises on class placement; his contribution will be to determine if a child's visual development is up to his chronological age.

Every school nurse will be provided with a simple device with which she can screen children for visual problems. That device does not exist today, but it could easily be designed and manufactured at minimal cost. Today all that nurse has is a Snellen chart. Every teacher will refer to the nurse for screening any child who is having trouble learning or who shows symptoms of a visual problem (see the list on pp. 57–58). If the screening shows there is a visual problem, the child will be referred to the vision consultant.

The result: the 75 percent of learning-disabled children who have visual problems will be treated, and treated early in their school history, before the problem has blighted their experience of education. In some cases, the therapy will be enough by itself to put the child back on the path of successful learning. For others, treatment will remove the visual roadblock and so make it possible for the child to benefit from other kinds of help. Children will not be asked to read before they are visually ready.

Vocational guidance will include consideration of vision. This kind of counselor, in concert with the school vision consultant, will suggest to high school students the kinds of career for which their vision is best suited. Students will be warned if they are considering a career in which their vision would prove a handicap. An example is a student with poor spatial perception who is thinking of taking up architecture. Such students will have the choice between seeking to improve those skills and changing their career plans.

The result: fewer young people will go into occupations in which a poorly adapted visual system will hold them back and afflict their lives with stress and unhappiness.

Every young person sent to prison (or other kinds of incarceration) will be screened for visual defects. Every prison rehabilitation program that includes schooling will also include vision treatment.

The result: a dramatic drop in the rate of repeat offenses by juveniles; less crime.

Employers will include vision in their plans. Vision consultants will help plan the workspace to minimize visual stress and maximize performance. All those who employ VDT operators will be required to put them in a place of work far different from today's visual sweatshops. VDT operators will get a short break every hour. Wellness programs for executives and other desk workers will include vision testing and, if needed, therapy to correct defects or enhance visual skills. Far-seeing employers will make such changes voluntarily because they know visually healthy workers make for a healthier balance sheet; shortsighted employers will be required to comply.

The result: a work force that is more productive because its members are less subject to absenteeism and below-par performance due to visual stress on the job.

Every state's automobile licensing system will require a much more extensive examination for the visual skills needed for safe driving. Here again, a simple device can be produced with which a lay person will screen applicants in no more than four or five minutes. Applicants who fail the test will be encouraged to improve their skills and try again. Students in high school driver-education courses will be similarly screened. In this case, treatment will be provided for those who need it. No student will pass driver education without the visual skills needed for licensing. Drivers who have reached the age at which visual skills diminish will be screened frequently and required to remedy, if possible, skills they have lost.

The result: fewer visually handicapped drivers, far fewer accidents and deaths on the highways.

Every sports team, from Little League to the Olympics, will have its vision consultant. Again, this will be a visually aware practitioner, not an "eyeball person." The Little League consultant will screen out children whose visual systems are still too immature for them to be playing. In high school and college, the consultant will screen out young people whose visual systems make them particularly prone to injury. At all levels, the consultant will help young people perform better as well as more safely. Consultants to professional teams will show athletes how to minimize risk while maximizing performance. Nowhere is such expert advice so needed as on state boxing commissions. Boxers need frequent visual screening, for a decline in, say, visual reaction time can expose a fighter to ring injuries that will leave him brain-damaged or even cause his death.

The result: better and safer athletic performance; better athletes and far fewer sports injuries all the way from grade school to Superbowl.

Professional schools—beginning with medical schools—whose graduates deal in any way with people's vision will add to their curricula courses in the development and functioning of vision so that no one will graduate without understanding that vision begins but does not end with the eyeball. In medical school, this is obviously most important in the case of ophthalmologists: the new kind of medical education will produce no more eye doctors who are ignorant of what we have learned about vision in the last fifty years. But it is also essential for pediatricians to understand the role vision plays in early childhood development, and, at the other end of the life-span, for geriatric specialists to know it is no longer true that "nothing can be done" for older people whose vision has diminished through the natural process of aging. Schools of education will make sure that future teachers know how vision affects the process of learning.

The result: eye doctors will provide for people's visual needs because they do not share the ignorant fatalism of today's practitioners; young children's visual needs will be diagnosed and treated before they confront the demands of school; older people will be able to lead more active and happier lives because they will no longer suffer from unnecessary visual handicaps.

We foresee other changes that will result from people's greater understanding of the needs of human vision. Toy and game manufacturers, for example, will design their products to stimulate visual skills rather than, as is too often the case today, depriving children of the opportunity to learn because the device does the visual tasks for them. Another example is in the design and arrangement of the home. Visually aware parents will arrange an infant's world to stimulate, not restrict, the growth of his visual skills. Builders of geriatric communities will design living spaces in ways—stronger lighting and color contrast, to name just two—that are most suited to people with aging vision. Many other changes will come as a result of heightened awareness.

Such is our vision of the visually aware society. The cost will be minimal. The payoff will be enormous. The time to start is now.

TAKING CARE OF YOUR EYES:
THE RIGHT READING CONDITIONS
AND THE RIGHT NUTRITION

That the modern world makes ever-growing demands on our visual systems has been a central theme of this book. It is all the more imperative, then, that we take good care of the eyes that are our windows on that world.

Here we offer suggestions in two areas that are particularly important to people who use their eyes intensively. One set of suggestions has to do with how we arrange our work and reading space, at home and, for those who have any control over it, on the job. The second topic we discuss is nutrition, and here our emphasis is on the relation of vitamins and minerals to vision.

LIGHTING AND ARRANGING
THE WORK AREA

Natural light is best. It is, after all, historically the light under which our eyes developed, and, until recent times, just about the only light they knew. Few of us, however, are able to do our desk work out of doors. At one time fluorescent lighting was thought to be an acceptable substitute for the real thing because it contained all the visible parts of the spectrum. A chance observation suggested that the omission of the invisible spectrum was potentially harmful. Photographer John Ott discovered this while doing time-lapse photography of plants; the plants suffered when they got only fluorescent light. Later research showed that prolonged exposure to fluorescent light can in fact do harm to people as well as plants. Ott then devoted himself to developing a fluorescent light that includes the "blacklight," the invisible part of the spectrum.

Full-spectrum fluorescent lighting is now commercially available. Acme Dunbar Industries makes a complete fixture that includes General Electric Chrome #50 tubes; other full-spectrum tubes include Vita-Lite, made by

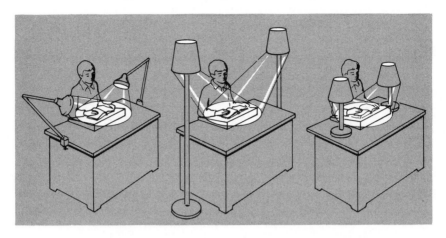

THREE WAYS TO LIGHT A DESK

Duro-Test, and Verilux, made by Verilux, Inc. Since the blacklight element wears out relatively soon, at least one manufacturer, Garcy Lighting, makes a separate blacklight tube, called Spectralite, that can be changed as needed without changing the main tube. Technology changes rapidly; the essential thing is to use full-spectrum if possible.

Avoid any kind of solid covering—it's usually plastic—over the source of light. This will screen out some parts of the light so that it is no longer full-spectrum. An "eggcrate" shield made of metal or plastic will protect the tube while letting through the essential light. Or else the tubes can be left exposed.

Overhead lighting, if possible with two or four fluorescent tubes, provides the best general illumination. In lighting the room in which you work, the general principle is moderation. The lighting should be medium, not bright but not pitch-dark, and there should be enough contrast to avoid monotony but not so much as to be distracting. The overhead light should be from 150 to 200 watts, supplementary lighting in the room 75 to 150 watts.

Floor lamps, as shown in the diagram above, are best for lighting your work area, whether desk or table. Whatever kind of lamp you use, it is best to have two, one on each side of the desk. Among desk lamps, the clamp-on type gives greater adaptability. Your aim is to have the reading area well but not excessively lit (so avoid high-intensity lamps); too much light is as hard on the eyes as too little. People vary in their needs for light. As a rough rule of thumb, 150 watts is about right for a standing lamp, 100 watts for a lamp on the table by your chair, 75 for a desk or gooseneck lamp close to your work. Whatever the source of light, position it so that there is neither glare nor shadow on the work area. Avoid too much contrast on the surface of the desk. If the desk is dark and the paper light, you can diminish contrast with a light-colored blotter.

Posture is important. In the diagram on p. 172, note that the chair provides back support and that the person's feet are flat on the floor. What you are reading should be placed at what is called the "Harmon distance" from the eyes. This is the distance from the elbow to the first knuckle of the hand. What you are reading should be placed perpendicular to the eyes. An inclined plane can help do this. Reading stands and, for lap reading, lapboards are available that will provide the right angle to the eyes.

Frequent breaks are essential. These breaks can increase, not diminish, your capacity for work and therefore your productivity, as well as decrease the strain on your eyes. Anyone using a VDT particularly needs to take breaks, but so do people doing any kind of desk work or, for that matter, just sitting in an armchair reading after dinner. The frequency of the breaks is more important than their duration. No one should maintain close visual attention for an hour without taking a five-minute break, but it's also a relief to the eyes if occasionally during that hour you give them just a momentary interruption in their labor by gazing for a few seconds across the room or out the window. If your eyes begin to blur, try shifting your focus rapidly back and forth from near to far, between the page and a more distant object; the wall will do if you don't have a window to look out of. Remember that what your eyes need is a break in visual concentration, not mental attention. It's quite all right to keep thinking about your work during a break as long as your eyes do not have to remain focused at reading distance. On the other hand, it does the eyes no good if you use a break to read a magazine as a form of mental distraction. You've stopped working then, but your eyes haven't. Give *them* the break.

VITAMINS FOR VISION

Our eyes are particularly sensitive to what we eat and don't eat. They need more nutrition for their weight than most parts of our bodies, and any deficiency may manifest itself in trouble of one sort or another.

As a general rule, a diet that is right for one's overall health will also be right for the eyes. A good supply of protein is particularly important to the eyes in the earlier years of life. One study provided evidence that an adequate diet of animal protein can slow or stop the onset of myopia, which as we have seen strikes so many people in their first twenty years.

Some vitamins and minerals are especially important to the eyes. The

GOOD READING POSTURE

amount of vitamins consumed by the eyes will vary enormously according
to the demands made on them, and at the same time they are sensitive to
even slight deficiencies in their supply. These facts argue for making sure
the eyes are getting enough of these nutrients in addition to a good overall
diet. Bear in mind that the Recommended Daily Allowances (RDA) are only
minimums needed to prevent disease, and that many nutrition specialists
believe that we and our eyes will benefit from substantially larger amounts.
We note in passing the unfortunate fact that little of the new knowledge
about the importance of nutrition to human performance has found its way
into health-care education.

Our purpose here is to discuss those vitamins and minerals in relation
to the eyes. We also note the foods richest in those substances. Those
who observe symptoms of deficiencies in their eyes may want to alter
their diet or vitamin intake, or both, to make sure their eyes are properly
nourished.

VITAMIN A. Known as the "eye vitamin," A is, along with D, the vitamin most necessary to our eyes.   ›

A form of vitamin A is one of the two main components (protein is the
other) in a substance in the retina called visual purple. Visual purple is used
in the process by which the retina transforms light into electrical impulses

sent to the brain. Messages of bright, contrasting light—a car's headlights at night, for example—consume visual purple. After each such message, the body must supply more vitamin A to keep the visual purple functioning. Any visual activity that exposes the eyes to harsh, glaring light will increase the demand for vitamin A. Driving at night is one example. Others are watching television, skiing, and spending time at a sunny beach or out on the water.

Night blindness is the most obvious signal that the eyes are not getting enough vitamin A. This will be noticeable when driving at night if you feel your vision is slow to recover after being temporarily blinded by another car's headlights. Or you may find it unusually hard to see in the uncertain light of sunset. Or adjusting to the sudden darkness of a movie theater takes longer than it used to. The eyes tire easily at night, and sometimes one sees dark spots that are not there.

Current research indicates that 20 percent of Americans show the visual symptoms of chronic deficiency in vitamin A. This can have serious consequences for the eyes. The lack of vitamin A depletes the mucous membrane of the tissues of the eyes, leaving them prone to the invasion of bacteria. One result is conjunctivitis ("pinkeye"): eyes that are itchy, inflamed, burning. Another is dryness of the cornea—"dry eyes." Untreated, this can lead to destruction of the cornea and blindness.

Some evidence indicates that vitamin A is more useful to the eyes when taken with small amounts of zinc.

Vitamin A is abundant in fish, meat, and poultry, and most of all in liver. Milk (whole, not skim), butter, and egg yolks are good sources. Vegetables contain carotene, a substance from which the body makes vitamin A. Good sources of carotene among vegetables include leafy vegetables (the darker the better), carrots, tomatoes, sweet potatoes, and turnips, and, among fruits, apricots.

THE B VITAMINS. These too provide important nourishment to the eyes. Deficiencies of the B vitamins manifest themselves as excessive sensitivity to the bright light of the sun, eyes that are bloodshot or burning or watery, or blind or dark spots in the vision. Insufficient B_1 (thiamine) can result in dry or burning eyes, unclear or double vision, nystagmus (involuntary jiggling of the eyes), and pain behind the eyeball. Lack of B_2 (riboflavin) can result in burning or itching eyes, reduced acuity, sensitivity to light, or the infiltration of blood vessels into the cornea. Some evidence indicates that the absence of B_2 may contribute to the development of cataracts, and that restoring the supply of this and other B vitamins can slow the cataract process in its early stages.

Insufficient B_{12} can cause difficulty in focusing or scotoma (loss of central vision). Other results can be a dimming of vision, headaches, trouble telling red from green. Smoking consumes a lot of vitamin B_{12}. Coffee and sugar also are large consumers of all the B vitamins.

Foods rich in the B vitamins include eggs, liver, whole grains, sunflower seeds, nuts, brewer's yeast, wheat germ.

VITAMIN C. A healthy lens has a rich supply of vitamin C, while a diseased lens, as in cases of glaucoma or cataract, has much less C. Lack of C can cause a sudden onset of exophthalmus (bulging eyes). Vitamin C has been found useful in treating glaucoma and diabetes, which leaves its victims prone to cataracts.

Most fresh fruits contain vitamin C, but it is most abundant in the citrus family: orange, grapefruit, lemon, lime. Tomato juice contains C. Watercress and cabbage are also good sources, but only if eaten raw or cooked quickly in little or no water.

VITAMIN D AND CALCIUM. We get vitamin D directly from the light of the sun. It functions in conjunction with calcium, the mineral needed by muscles and bones.

Evidence is accumulating that vitamin D and calcium deficiencies contribute to myopia, and that restoring an adequate supply can slow or stop the onset of nearsightedness. It appears to do this by removing excess liquid from the eyeball. As we saw in Chapter 10, too much liquid pressure in the eyeball causes myopia by pushing the lens forward so that the image does not fall clearly on the retina. Reducing the amount of liquid lessens the pressure that stretches the eyeball out of shape. Several studies have shown that myopic children are often deficient in calcium.

Dr. Arthur Knapp, an ophthalmologist at the Columbia University College of Physicians and Surgeons, has used vitamin D and calcium in treating patients suffering from eye ailments that most often come with age: cataract, retinitis pigmentosa, detached retina, glaucoma. Knapp has also used the same combination successfully in treating myopia. In treating patients whose myopia was increasing, he found that the vitamin-D-and-calcium treatment slowed the rate of increase in half the patients. One-third of the same group found that their nearsightedness was decreased after the treatment. What happens is that the vitamin-mineral combination dehydrates the outer tissue of the eye and thus reduces the elongation of the eyeball that causes myopia.

The light of the sun is by far the most important source of vitamin D. The foods that are rich in vitamin A also contain D, but not in the amount necessary to substitute for sunlight. Whole milk, cheese, raw vegetables, salmon, sardines, almonds, and oats are all good sources of calcium.

VITAMIN E. This vitamin, which helps new blood vessels to form, is useful in slowing the diminishing of vision that so often comes with advancing years. One study, in Italy, found that an added supply of vitamin E reversed presbyopia (the blurred near vision that comes with age) in patients past forty. Vitamin E nourishes the connective tissues of the eyes. The stronger this tissue is, the better it can resist the pressure that near-point work puts on the size of the eyeball. This too can help stave off myopia.

Wheat germ is the most abundant source of vitamin E. Leafy green vegetables, eggs, and nuts are also good sources.

CHROMIUM. Recent research suggests that a deficiency in this mineral contributes to the development of myopia. One study showed that children who were becoming myopic had one-third the supply of chromium of comparable children who were not becoming nearsighted.

Foods that provide chromium include corn oil, meat, whole grains, brewer's yeast, and the sweet and starchy vegetables and fruits.

APPENDIX B
RESEARCH ON VISION THERAPY

Vision therapy in its many aspects has been the subject of a vast amount of scholarly study. What follows is a summary of major research findings on the main topics covered in this book, with references for those who may want to explore the subject still further.

VISION AND LEARNING DISABILITY

A number of studies have shown the high correlation between visual disorders and reading problems and other kinds of learning disability. (It should be noted here that these visual disorders do not include refractive error or eye disease. Other studies have shown little or no correlation between those problems and learning disability.)

Seiderman (1980) found that 73 percent of a learning-disabled population also were deficient in visual skills. Hoffman (1980) examined the vision and visual-perceptual skills of 107 learning-disabled children from five to fourteen years old. In their vision skills, he found high percentages of the children deficient in the areas tested: binocular coordination (87 percent), focus ability (64 percent), focus facility (83 percent), ocular motor efficiency (94 percent). In perceptual skills, he found them deficient as follows: bilateral integration (46 percent), directionality (74 percent), visual discrimination (50 percent), figure-ground (53 percent), visualization (73 percent), visual-motor integration (81 percent), auditory perceptual discrimination and integration (44 percent). These percentages were more than twice as high in each category as the rate found among other children who were patients in the same optometry clinic but were not reported to have learning problems.

Other researchers have studied the relationship between learning disability and particular visual skills. Marcus (1974) found that only four of sixty learning-disabled children scored 70 percent or more of normal in total binocular efficiency. More important, the study revealed a syndrome of visual deficiencies, finding that learning-disabled children suffered from reduced convergence and fusion ability at reading distance, poor focusing flexibility, and poor fixation and eye-tracking skills. Benton et al. (1972) found 77 percent of 115 learning-disabled children deficient in binocular control, and Sherman (1973) reported 92 percent of a similar population deficient in binocular fusion. In eye-movement skills, Sherman (1973) found 96 percent of learning-disabled children deficient in ocular-motor efficiency, and Woolf (1969) found 70 percent to have poor tracking abilities. Pavlidis (1981) found significantly poorer eye-movement patterns among dyslexic children. Beltman et al. (1967) found that 54 percent of poor readers were unable to follow smoothly a diagonally moving target, compared to 11 percent of a control group. In the ability to focus, both Sherman (1973) and Woolf (1969) found more than 70 percent of learning-disabled children deficient.

In the area of perceptual skills, Birch and Belmont (1965) reported that reading readiness correlated more closely with auditory-visual integration than with IQ. Silver (1961) found that nine of ten children with reading disabilities had deficits in visual perception, especially in figure-ground perception. Other researchers reported figure-ground deficiencies among learning-disabled children (Ayres, 1969; Cruikshank, 1967; Eisenberg, 1966; Seiderman, 1972; Silver, 1961; Solan and Seiderman, 1970). In visual directionality, Sherman (1973) and Seiderman (1973) found that 76–78 percent of learning-disabled children experienced difficulty. Woolf (1960) reported that 60 percent of a similar population failed a directionality test. In visual-motor skills, Silver and Hagin (1967) reported that 92 percent of a dyslexic population showed deficits. Sherman (1973) showed a 92 percent incidence of eye-hand coordination problems among learning-disabled children. Similar findings have been reported by Ilg and Ames (1966) and Koppitz (1966). Valuable studies in this field, including all those cited above, are:

Atzmon, D. Positive effect of improving relative fusional vergence on reading and learning disabilities. *Binocular Vision*, 1985, I, 39–43.

Ayres, A. J. Deficits in sensory integration in educationally handicapped children. *Journal of Learning Disabilities*, 1969, 2, 160–168.

Beltman, J. W.; Stern, E. L.;

Whitsell, L. J.; and Gofman, H. E. Cerebral dominance in developmental dyslexia. *Archives of Ophthalmology*, 1967, 78, 722–729.

Benton, C. D., Jr.; McCann, J. W.; and Larson, M. A practical approach for the ophthalmologist. *Journal of Pediatric Ophthalmology*, 1972, 5, 25–29.

Birch, H. G., and Belmont, L. Auditory-visual integration, intelligence and reading ability in school-children. *Perceptual Motor Skills*, 1965, 20, 295–305.

Cruikshank, W. M. *The brain-injured child in home, school and community*. New York: Syracuse University Press, 1967.

Eisenberg, L. The management of the hyperkinetic child. *Developmental Medicine and Child Neurology*, 1966, 8, 593–598.

Forrest, E. Visual imagery as an information processing strategy. *Journal of Learning Disabilities*, 1981, 14, 584–586.

Haddad, H., et al. The use of orthoptics in dyslexia. *Journal of Learning Disabilities*, 1983, 17, 141–144.

Hoffman, L. G. Incidence of vision difficulties in children with learning disabilities. *Journal of the American Optometric Association*, 1980, 51, 447–451.

Ilg, F., and Ames, L. B. *School readiness*. New York: Harper & Row, 1966.

Koppitz, E. *The Bender-Gestalt Test for young children*. New York: Grune & Stratton, 1966.

Ludlam, W. Visual electrophysiology and reading/learning difficulties. *Journal of Learning Disabilities*, 1981, 14, 587–590.

Marcus, S. A syndrome of visual constrictions in the learning-disabled child. *Journal of the American Optometric Association*, 1974, 45, 6.

Pavlidis, G. Do eye movements hold the key to dyslexia? *Neuropsychologia*, 1981, 19, 57–64.

Seiderman, A. S. A look at perceptual-motor training. *Academic Therapy*, 1972, 7, 315–321.

———. An optometric approach to the diagnosis of visually based problems in learning. In Gerald Leisman, ed., *Basic Visual Processes and Learning Disability*. Springfield, Ill.: Charles C. Thomas, 1976.

———. Optometric vision therapy—results of a demonstration project with a learning disabled population. *Journal of the American Optometric Association*, 1980, 51, 489–493.

———. Preliminary findings of a program of optometric vision therapy in an academic environment. Paper presented at the Gesell Institute of Child Development, New Haven, Conn., June 1973.

———. Guest Editor. *Journal of Learning Disabilities*, 1981, 14.

Sherman, A. Relating vision disorders to learning disability. *Journal of the American Optometric Association*, 1973, 44, 140–141.

Silver, A. A. Diagnostic considerations in children with learning disability. *Bulletin Orton Society*, 1961, 11, 91.

Silver, A. A., and Hagin, R. A. Strategies of intervention in the spectrum of defects in specific reading disability. *Bulletin Orton Society*, 1967, 11, 91.

Solan, H. A. A rationale for the optometric treatment and management of children with learning disabilities. *Journal of Learning Disabilities*, 1981, 14, 568–572.

Solan, H. A., and Seiderman, A. S. Case report on a grade one child before and after perceptual-motor training. *Journal of Learning Disabilities*, 1970, 3, 635–639.

Wachs, H. Visual implications of Piaget's theory of cognitive development. *Journal of Learning Disabilities*, 1981, 14, 581–583.

Woolf, D. Dyschriesopia: A syndrome of visual disability. In R. M. Wold, ed., *Visual and perceptual aspects for the achieving and underachieving child*. Seattle: Special Child Publications, 1969.

THE EFFECT OF VISION THERAPY ON READING AND LEARNING

The research literature in this field is enormous. Over the years, but mostly since the mid-1960s, many hundreds of studies have been published, ranging from individual case reports to research projects covering large numbers of schoolchildren and college students. Here we will cite only surveys that summarize the results of this work.

The first major survey was by Steven B. Greenspan (Research Studies of Visual & Perceptual-Motor Training. Continuing Education Course, vol. 44. Santa Ana, Calif.: Optometric Extension Program Foundation, 1972). Greenspan analyzed a total of 111 studies by eighty authors and groups of authors who reported on the effect of vision therapy on reading and learning skills. The number of children or students reported on ranged from fewer than ten in six studies to more than fifty each in twenty-five studies. Kindergarten children were investigated in twenty-six studies, first graders in twenty-eight, older elementary schoolchildren in forty-four, and high school students, college students, and adults in twenty-seven studies.

Greenspan combined the figures given in all the studies and calculated that 72 percent of the results reported were successful, 15 percent were unsuccessful, and 13 percent were successful by some of the criteria used. He then eliminated those studies that he considered flawed in their design or analysis. This yielded these results: 74 percent successful, 20 percent unsuccessful, and 6 percent partially successful.

Since 1974, the *Journal of Optometric Vision Development* has published, usually in its March issue, an "Annual Review of Literature in Developmental Optometry." The authors review papers and research studies ranging in number from 167 to more than 300. Of these, from one-quarter to one-third are related to vision and its impact on learning and reading.

In its issue for February 1988 (59:95–105), the *Journal of the American Optometric Association* published a special report on "The Efficacy of Optometric Vision Therapy." This report covers 238 papers, of which many are concerned with the efficacy of vision therapy in solving reading and learning problems.

VISION THERAPY AND SPECIFIC DISORDERS

STRABISMUS. Strabismus was the first visual disorder treated with vision therapy, or orthoptics, as it was then called. Thus it has long been a subject of research. We will limit ourselves here to studies made in recent years, when the techniques in use were largely those practiced today.

All the studies reported functional cure rates of at least 50 percent. The majority reported success rates over 70 percent, and for the most prevalent forms of strabismus the rates reported are sometimes over 90 percent. ("Functional cure" means that the patient after therapy has full binocular vision. This is in contrast to "cosmetic cure," which means only that the eyes now appear properly aligned but do not necessarily work together as a team.)

Marcus (1985) reported on the results of vision therapy with 150 patients of ages ranging from six years on up. Of these, seventy-six were esotropes (eyes turned in), fifty-nine exotropes (eyes turned out), and fifteen had a vertical imbalance.

The overall rate of cure (functional as well as cosmetic) was 76 percent. Exotropes were most successful, with 88 percent cured, followed by esotropes, 68 percent, and verticals, 55 percent. Thirty-six patients suffered from anomalous retinal correspondence, a disorder which responds much less well to vision therapy than do other forms of strabismus. If they are excluded from the totals, the rates of cure rise to 96 percent for esotropes, 95 percent for exotropes, and 88 percent for verticals.

Marcus found that the highest rate of cure by age, 86 percent, was with patients nine to twelve years old. For those six to eight, it was 73 percent; for those thirteen to sixteen, 71 percent; and for those seventeen and over, including adults, the success rate was 70 percent.

Marcus contrasted these results with those of surgery for strabismus. He cited studies of surgery reporting functional cure rates of, respectively, 40 percent, 11 percent, and 10 percent. Another study reported that 22 percent of those operated on experienced a cosmetic cure, while 78 percent were left without effective binocular vision.

In other studies of vision therapy and strabismus, Ludlam (1961) reported functional cures in 73 percent of 149 patients. In a follow-up study, Ludlam and Kleinman (1965) found that after three to seven years 81 percent of the patients had maintained their binocular vision, for an overall cure rate of 65 percent. The rate of cosmetic cure was 96 percent.

Flax and Duckman (1978), in a survey of research studies involving 489 patients, found a success rate of 86 percent. Etting (1978) found a functional cure rate of 71 percent. If patients suffering from anomalous retinal correspondence are excluded, the rate rises to 89 percent.

Kertesz and Kertesz (1986) reported a 74 percent rate of success among fifty-seven patients who worked with computer-generated stereo graphics in addition to the usual vision therapy.

Etting, G. Strabismus therapy in private practice: Cure rates after three months of therapy. *Journal of the American Optometric Association*, 1978, 49:1367–73.

Flax, N., and Duckman, R. H. Orthoptic treatment of strabismus. *Journal of the American Optometric Association*, 1978, 49:1353–61.

Kertesz, A. E., and Kertesz, J. Wide-field stimulation in strabismus. *American Journal of Optometry and Physiological Optics*, 1986, 63:217–22.

Ludlam, W. M. Orthoptic treatmentment of strabismus. *American Journal of Optometry and Physiological Optics*, 1961, 38:369–88.

Ludlam, W. M., and Kleinman, W. M. The long-range results of orthoptic treatment of strabismus. *American Journal of Optometry and Archives of American Academy of Optometry*, 1965, 42:647–84.

Marcus, S. Functional cure rate for strabismus. Research paper presented at optometric congresses in 1985.

CONVERGENCE INSUFFICIENCY. After strabismus, this is the most prevalent disorder of binocular vision. Researchers have reported a high rate of success in treating convergence insufficiency with vision therapy.

Cooper and Duckman (1978), in a review of previous research studies, found that 95 percent of the patients involved "responded favorably" to vision therapy.

Dalziel (1981) reported on one hundred patients who failed a standard measure known as Sheard's criterion. After vision therapy, eighty-four patients passed the same test. Discomfort and loss of efficiency were reported by eighty-three patients before the therapy, but only seven afterwards.

Pantano (1982), in a study of two hundred patients, found that the majority showed normal visual skills two years after vision therapy for convergence insufficiency. Daum (1984) reported similar results in a retrospective study of 110 patients.

Cooper, J., and Duckman, R. Convergence insufficiency: Incidence, diagnosis and treatment. *Journal of the American Optometric Association*, 1978, 49:673–680.

Dalziel, C. C. Effect of vision training on patients who fail Sheard's criterion. *American Journal of Optometry and Physiological Optics*, 1983, 60:982–989.

Daum, K. M. Convergence insufficiency. *American Journal of Optometry and Physiological Optics*, 1984, 61:16–22.

Pantano, R. Orthoptic treatment of convergence insufficiency: a two-year follow-up report. *American Orthoptic Journal*, 1982, 32:73–80.

MYOPIA. This of course is by far the most prevalent of eye problems. So it comes as no surprise that myopia has been the subject of a huge body of research. However, little of that research has been concerned with the link between myopia and reading, and the use of biofeedback in vision therapy for myopia is so new that not much has been published about it.

On the link to reading, Rosner and Belkin (1987) reported on a study of the vision scores of 157,748 Israelis aged seventeen to nineteen who had been screened for military service. They found that those with more schooling were more likely to be nearsighted, the incidence of myopia rising from 7.5 percent among those with eight or fewer years of school to 19.7 percent among those with twelve or more years. In the same paper the authors summarize the results of earlier studies that also showed a correlation between myopia and years in school.

Trachtman (1978, 1982) has described his use of biofeedback to reduce myopia. Trachtman (1985) reported results of biofeedback therapy with eighty-four patients. The patients' acuity before therapy ranged from 20/20 to 20/1000, with a median of 20/200. After an average of eight sessions of therapy the patients' acuity ranged from 20/15 to 20/200, with a median of 20/30.

Berman et al. (1985) reported, after using the Trachtman instrument for biofeedback therapy, that all of sixteen patients were less myopic after treatment and that the amount of reduction could be predicted.

On another aspect of myopia, prevention, Streff (1977) reported that two measures in the early grades—delaying reading instruction until the child's visual system is ready, and instituting a half-hour per day of vision-developing games—produced, in the sixth grade, a lower incidence of myopia as compared to a control group.

Berman, P., et al. The effectiveness of biofeedback visual training as a viable method of treatment and reduction of myopia. *Journal of Optometric Vision Development*, 1985, 16:17–21.

Rosner, M., and Belkin, M. Intelligence, education, and myopia in males. *Archives of Ophthalmology*, 1987, 105:1508–1511.

Streff, J. Changes in incidence of myopia following program of intervention. In Cool, S. J., and Smith, E. L., eds. *Frontiers in Visual Science*.

New York: Springer-Verlag, 1977.

Trachtman, J. Biofeedback of accommodation to reduce myopia: a case report. *American Journal of Optometry*, 1978, 55(6):400–406.

———. Myopia reduction by biofeedback training. Paper presented at the 1982 American Academy of Optometry Convention, Philadelphia.

———. Myopia reduction using biofeedback of accommodation: summary results of 100 patients. Paper presented at the National Eye Research Foundation, 1985, Hamilton, Bermuda.

VISION AND JUVENILE DELINQUENCY

Research studies have documented the high incidence of visual problems among juvenile delinquents. Other studies have shown that providing vision therapy to incarcerated juveniles results in a much lower rate of repeat offenses after they are released. The studies are:

Dowis, R. T. The importance of vision in the prevention of learning disabilities and juvenile delinquency. *Journal of Optometric Vision Development*, 1984, 15(3):20–22.

Dzik, D. Vision and the juvenile delinquent. *Journal of the American Optometric Association*, 1966, 37:461–468.

———. Optometric intervention in the control of juvenile delinquents. *Journal of the American Optometric Assocation*, 1975, 46:6.

Kaseno, S. Screening and treatment program for vision and learning disabilities among juvenile delinquents. *Curriculum II*, vol. 58, no. 7. Santa Ana, Calif.: Optometric Extension Program Foundation, 1986.

Zaba, J., and Bachara, G. H. Learning disabilities and juvenile delinquency: Beyond the correlation. *Journal of Learning Disabilities*, April 1978.

FOR FURTHER READING

Abrams, J. The psychologist-educator views the relationship to reading and related learning disabilities. *Journal of Learning Disabilities*, 1981, 14:565–567.

Ayres, A. Learning disabilities and the vestibular system. *Journal of Learning Disabilities*, 1978, 11:18–29.

Bach-y-rita, P., et al. Vision substitution by tactile image projection. *Nature*, 1969, 221:963.

Bachara, G., et al. Human figure

drawings and LD children. *Academic Therapy*, 1974–75, 10:151–158.

Belmont, I., et al. Comparison of perceptual training and remedial instruction for poor beginning readers. *Journal of Learning Disabilities*, 1973, 6:230–235.

Berner, G., and Berner, D. Relation of ocular dominance, handedness, and the controlling eye in binocular vision. *Archives of Ophthalmology*, 1953, 50:603–608.

Bettman, J., et al. Cerebral dominance in developmental dyslexia. *Archives of Ophthalmology*, 1967, 78:722–729.

Betts, E. A physiological approach to the analysis of reading difficulties. *Educational Research Bulletin*, 1974, 13:135–173.

Birnbaum, M. Clinical management of myopia. *American Journal of Optometry and Physiological Optics*, 1981, 58:554–559.

———. Esotropia, exotropia and cognitive/perceptual style. *Journal of the American Optometric Association*, 1981, 635–644.

Birnbaum, M., et al. Success in amblyopia therapy as a function of age. *American Journal of Optometry and Physiological Optics*, 1977, 54:269–275.

Birnbaum, P., and Birnbaum, M. Binocular coordination as a factor in reading achievement. *Journal of the American Optometric Association*, 1968, 39:48–56.

Blum, H., et al. Vision screening for elementary schools: the Orinda study. Berkeley: University of California Press, 1959.

Bobier, W., and Sivak, J. Orthoptic treatment of subjects showing slow accommodative response. *American Journal of Optometry and Archives of American Academy of Optometry*, 1983, 60:678–87.

Calaroso, E. After-image transfer: a therapeutic procedure for amblyopia. *American Journal of Optometry and Archives of American Academy of Optometry*, 1972, 49:65–69.

Carter, J. Predictable visual responses to increasing age. *Journal of the American Optometric Association*, 1982, 53:31–36.

Chernick, B. Profile of peripheral visual anomalies in the disabled reader. *Journal of the American Optometric Association*, 1978, 49:1117–1118.

Cohen, A. Monocular fixation in a binocular field. *Journal of the American Optometric Association*, 1981, 52:801–806.

Cohen, B., et al. Do hyperactive children have manifestations of hyperactivity of eye movements? *Journal of Optometric Vision Development*, 1976, 7:18.

———. An optometric approach to the rehabilitation of the stroke patient. *Journal of the American Optometric Association*, 52:795–800.

Coleman, H. Visual perception and reading dysfunction. *Journal of Learning Disabilities*, 1968, 1(2):116–123.

———. The West Warwick visual perception study. *Journal of the American Optometric Association*, 43:452–462 and 532–543.

Cooper, J. Treatment of a decompensating strabismic who had diplo-plia and vertex headaches. *Journal of the American Optometric Association,* 1977, 48:1557–1558.

Cooper, J., and Baron, S. Treatment of a divergence excess and amblyopia with orthoptic training and contact lens. *Journal of the American Optometric Association,* 1974, 45:743–745.

Cooper, J., et al. Reduction of asthenopia in patients with convergence insufficiency after fusional vergence training. *American Journal of Optometry and Archives of American Academy of Optometry,* 1983, 60:982–989.

Cooper, J., and Feldman, J. Operant conditioning of fusional convergence ranges using random dot stereograms. *American Journal of Optometry and Archives of American Academy of Optometry,* 1980, 57:205–213.

Cowden, J., and Bores, L. A clinical investigation of the surgical correction of myopia by the method of Fyodorov. *American Academy of Ophthalmology,* 1981, 737–741.

Critchley, M. *Developmental dyslexia.* London: William Heinemann Medical Books, 1964.

Daum, K. Accommodative insufficiency. *American Journal of Optometry and Archives of American Academy of Optometry,* 1983, 60:352–359.

Davis, M. A pilot project to study the effects of enhancing visual function, visually guided mobility, and visually guided coordination on independence in the elderly. *Journal of Optometric Vision Development,* 1984, 15:23–26.

DeQuiros, J. Diagnosis of vestibular disorders in the learning disabled. *Journal of Learning Disabilities,* 1976, 9:39–47.

Duckman, R. Effectiveness of vision therapy on a population of cerebral palsy children. *Journal of the American Optometric Association,* 1980, 51:607–614.

Dunsing, J. Perceptual motor factors in the development of school reading and analysis of the Purdue perceptual-motor survey. *American Journal of Optometry and Archives of American Academy of Optometry,* 1969, 46:760–765.

Eames, T. Comparison of eye conditions among 1,000 reading failures, 500 ophthalmic patients, and 150 unselected children. *American Journal of Ophthalmology,* 1948, 31:713–717.

———. The effect of anisometropia on reading achievement. *American Journal of Optometry and Archives of American Academy of Optometry,* 1964, 41:700–702.

Ebersole, M., et al. *Steps to achievement for the slow learner.* Columbus, Ohio: Merrill, 1968.

Flax, N., et al. Symposium: is there a relationship between vision therapy and academic achievement? Part II. *Review of Optometry,* 1977, 114:44–52.

Flom, M. Corresponding and disparate retinal points in normal and anomalous correspondence. *Ameri-*

can *Journal of Optometry and Physiological Optics*, 1980, 57:656–665.

―――. Prevalence of amblyopia. *American Journal of Optometry and Archives of American Academy of Optometry*, 1966, 73:732–751.

Gesell, A., et al. *Vision, its development in infant and child*. New York: Paul B. Hoeber, 1949.

Getman, G. *To develop your child's intelligence*. Luverne, Minn.: Getman, 1962.

―――. *Techniques and diagnostic criteria for the optometric care of children's vision*. Duncan, Okla.: Optometric Extension Program, 1959.

Getz, D. Vision and sports. *Journal of the American Optometric Association*, 1978, 49:385–388.

Gottlieb, D., and Powers, L. The visual and visual motor integrative space-span perceptual welding screening. *Journal of the American Optometric Association*, 52:651–653.

Greenspan, S. Research studies of bifocals for myopia. *American Journal of Optometry and Physiological Optics*, 1981, 58:536–540.

Grisham, J. The dynamics of fusional vergence eye movements in binocular dysfunction. *American Journal of Optometry and Physiological Optics*, 1980, 57:645–655.

Halliwell, J., and Solan, H. The effects of a supplemental perceptual training program on first grade reading achievement. *Exceptional Children*, 1972, 38:613–621.

Henson, D., and North, R. Adaptation to prism-induced heterophoria. *American Journal of Optometry*

and *Physiological Optics*, 1980, 57:129–137.

Hoffman, L., et al. Effectiveness of optometric therapy for strabismus in a private practice. *American Journal of Optometry and Archives of American Academy of Optometry*, 1970, 47:990–995.

Hoffman, L., and Rouse, M. Referral recommendations for binocular function and/or developmental perceptual deficiencies. *Journal of the American Optometric Association*, 1980, 51:119–126.

Kavner, R. Corrective therapy for amblyopia and esotropia. *Review of Optometry*, 1980, 117:57–58.

Kephart, N., et al. Vision and achievement in kindergarten. *American Journal of Optometry and Archives of American Academy of Optometry*, 1960, 37:36–39.

Kirschner, A. A comparison of eye movement and eye-hand coordination scores between normal school children and perceptual handicapped. *Journal of the American Optometric Association*, 1967, 38:561–566.

Kirshen, D., and Flom, M. Visual acuity at different retinal loci of eccentrically fixating functional amblyopes. *American Journal of Optometry and Physiological Optics*, 1978, 55:144–150.

Kundel, H., and Nodine, C. Studies of eye movements and visual search in radiology. In Senders, J., et al., eds. *Eye movements and higher psychological functioning*. Hillsdale, N.J.: Lawrence Erlbaum Assoc., 1978.

Lane, B. A7 folate, ascorbate, calcium, chromium, and vanadium in myopia prevention and reversal. *Metabolic, Pediatric, and Systematic Ophthalmology*, 1982, 6:149–150.

Letourneau, J., and Ludlam, W. Biofeedback reinforcement in the training of limitation of gaze: a case report. *American Journal of Optometry and Physiological Optics*, 1976, 53:672–676.

Lindquist, G. Preschool screening as a means of predicting later reading achievement. *Journal of Learning Disabilities*, 1982, 15:331–332.

Liu, J., et al. Objective assessment of accommodation orthoptics: dynamic insufficiency. *American Journal of Optometry and Physiological Optics*, 1979, 56:285–291.

Locher, P., and Worms, P. Visual scanning strategies of perceptually impaired and normal children viewing the motor-free visual perception test. *Journal of Learning Disabilities*, 1981, 14:416–419.

Ludlam, W. Visual electrophysiology and reading/learning difficulties. *Journal of Learning Disabilities*, 1981, 14:587–590.

———. Visual training, the alpha activation cycle and reading. *Journal of the American Optometric Association*, 1979, 50:111–115.

Ludlam, W., et al. Optometric visual training for reading disability: a case report. *American Journal of Optometry and Archives of American*

Academy of Optometry, 1973, 50:58–66.

Marcus, S. A syndrome of visual restriction in the learning-disabled child. *Journal of the American Optometric Association*, 1974, 46:746–749.

McKee, G. The role of the optometrist in the development of perceptual and visuomotor skills in children. *American Journal of Optometry and Archives of American Academy of Optometry*, 1967, 5:297–310.

Mohindra, J. Appendix to Convergence Insufficiency. *Optometric Monthly*, 1980, 71:463–466.

Morgan, M. *The effect of visual perceptual training upon subsequent scholastic progress of children with specific visual disabilities*. Duncan, Okla.: Optometric Extension Program Foundation, 1968.

Ott, J. Influence of fluorescent lights on hyperactivity and learning disabilities. *Journal of Learning Disabilities*, 1976, 8:417–422.

Park, G., and Burri, C. The relationship of various eye conditions and reading achievement. *Journal of Educational Psychology*, 1943, 34:290–299.

Pasquale, D., et al. The birthday effect. *Journal of Learning Disabilities*, 1980, 13:234–238.

Piaget, J. *The mechanisms of perception*. New York: Basic Books, 1969.

Pierce, J. Reading disability: the result of a basic vision function problem. *Review of Optometry*, 1979, 116:43.

———. Improving visual skills in

a double hypertrope. *Review of Optometry*, 1978, 115:42–43.

Pirozzolo, F. Eye movements and reading disability. In Rayner K., ed. *Eye movements in reading: Perceptual and language processes.* New York: Academic Press, 1983.

Pollatsek, A. What can eye movements tell us about dyslexia? In Rayner, K., ed. *Eye movements in reading: Perceptual and language processes.* New York: Academic Press, 1983.

Punnett, A., et al. Relationship between reinforcement and eye movements during ocular motor training with learning disabled children. *Journal of Learning Disabilities*, 1984, 17:16–9.

Quere, M., and Pechereau, A. Surgical results in functional squints. *Ophthalmologica*, 1981, 104–112.

Richman, J. Use of a sustained visual attention task to determine children at risk for learning problems. *Journal of the American Optometric Association*, 1986, 57:20–26.

Robertson, E. The visual guidance program: evaluation report. *Journal of the American Optometric Association*, 1977, 48:915–919.

Robinson, H. Factors related to monocular and binocular reading efficiency. *American Journal of Optometry and Archives of American Academy of Optometry*, 1951, 28:337–346.

Rosner, J. A procedure for measuring the near-point fusional reserves of young children. *Journal of*

the American Optometric Association, 1979, 49:473–474.

Rowsey, J., et al. Preliminary report of Los Alamos keratoplasty. *American Academy of Ophthalmology*, 1981, 755–760.

Ryan, P. *The Cambrian project.* Final report for project no., 43-69384-3526424, California State Department of Education, 1973.

Schrock, R. Research relating vision and learning. In Wold, R., ed. *Vision: its impact on learning.* Seattle: Special Child Publications, 1978.

Seiderman, A. Motor planning and developmental apraxia. *Journal of the American Optometric Association*, 1970, 41:846–857.

———. Results of a program of optometric vision therapy within an academic environment. Paper presented at the annual meeting of the College of Optometrists in Vision Development, San Francisco, October 29, 1975.

———. Results of a program of visual and perceptual training within an academic environment. Paper presented at the annual meeting of the American Academy of Optometry, section on Binocular Vision and Perception, Miami Beach, Fla., December 15, 1974.

———. Visual function assessment. In Adamson, W., and Adamson, K., eds. *A handbook for specific learning disabilities.* New York: Gardner Press, 1979.

Selenow, S., and Ciufredda K. Vision function recovery during orthoptic therapy in an adult amblyope. *Journal of the American Optometric Association*, 1986, 57:132–140.

Solan, H. Visual processing training with the tachistoscope: a rationale and grade one norms. *Journal of Learning Disabilities*, 1969, 2:30–37.

Solan, H., et al. The relationship of perceptual-motor development to learning readiness in kindergarten: a multivariate analysis. *Journal of Learning Disabilities*, 1985, 18:3437–3444.

Suchoff, I. Visual development. *Journal of the American Optometric Association*, 1979, 50:1129–1135.

Taylor, E. The spans: perception, apprehension and recognition. *American Journal of Ophthalmology*, 1957, 44:501–507.

Tyler, R. Looking and seeing: their relation to visual cognition. *Neuro-Ophthalmology*, 1968, 4:249–265.

Vrana, F., and Pihl, R. Selective attention deficit in L.D. children: a cognitive interpretation. *Journal of Learning Disabilities*, 1980, 13:387–391.

Walker, R., and Streff, J. A perceptual program for classroom teachers: some results. *Genetic Psychology Monographs*, 1973, 87:253–288.

Warshowsky, J. A vision screening of a Down's syndrome population. *Journal of the American Optometric Association*, 1981, 52:605–607.

Weber, G. Visual disabilities—their identification with academic achievement. *Journal of Learning Disabilities*, 1980, 13:13–19.

Wesson, M. Prism for esotropia. *Review of Optometry*, 1980, 10:44–48.

Wick, B. Vision training for presbyopic non-strabismic patients. *American Journal of Optometry and Physiological Optics*, 1977, 54:244–247.

Wold, R., et al. Effectiveness of optometric vision therapy. *Journal of the American Optometric Association*, 1978, 49:1047–1054.

Zaba, J., et al. Visual data of low ranked college freshmen. *Optometric Weekly*, 1974, 65:415–417.

INDEX

A NOTE ABOUT THE AUTHORS

Dr. Arthur S. Seiderman is a doctor of optometry who has also earned a masters degree in psychology, and practices in Philadelphia. He is president of the Disabled Reader Group of the International Reading Association as well as the president-elect of the Multidisciplinary Academy of Clinical Education. Dr. Seiderman's book *The Athletic Eye* was the first major work ever written on the subject of vision and the athlete. He has taught graduate courses in learning disabilities at Pennsylvania State University (Ogontz campus) for many years. Dr. Seiderman, who is a Fellow of the American Academy of Optometry, serves on the editorial advisory board of the *Journal of Learning Disabilities*. His work has been translated into five languages and he has lectured throughout the United States, Canada, and Europe and has been published widely in journals. He is president and co-founder of the Sports Vision Center of Philadelphia, and has served as a vision consultant to the Philadelphia Flyers. He lives with his wife and three children in Philadelphia.

Dr. Steven E. Marcus is a doctor of optometry and co-founder and co-director of the Sports Vision Center of Philadelphia. He is, in addition, founder and director of the Sports Vision Center of Valley Forge, Pennsylvania, and the founder and president of the Binocular Vision Centers. Dr. Marcus has lectured at different universities on perception and learning and has served as a vision consultant for the U.S. Olympic team. He practices optometry in Pennsylvania, where he lives with his wife and three children.

David Hapgood was a writer at the *New York Times* and is the author or co-author of several books, most recently *The Murder of Napoleon* and *Monte Cassino*.

A NOTE ON THE TYPE

The text of this book was set in a digitized version of Janson, a typeface thought to
have been made by the Dutchman Anton Janson, who was practicing type founder
in Leipzig during the years 1668–1687. However, it has been conclusively demonstrated that these types are actually the work of Nicholas Kis (1650–1702), a
Hungarian, who most probably learned his trade from the master Dutch type
founder Dirk Voskens. The type is an example of the influential and sturdy Dutch
types that prevailed in England up to the time William Caslon developed his own
designs from them.

Composed by
Dix Type Inc., Syracuse, New York

Printed and bound by
Murray Printing Company, Westford, Massachusetts

Designed by Iris Weinstein